THE NEW POLITICS

THE NEW POLITICS

*The Expanding Technology of
Political Manipulation*

by

JAMES M. PERRY

 Clarkson N. Potter, Inc./Publisher   NEW YORK

DISTRIBUTED BY CROWN PUBLISHERS, INC.

Table of Contents

FOREWORD

THIS BOOK GROWS OUT OF SOME SIX YEARS of political reporting for the *National Observer*. It is, however, my book, re-
flecting my own thoughts and opinions and biases. Whatever
its merits or faults, they are mine and not my employers.

There would, however, be no book if it were not for
the indulgence of my editors. During most of the time I
reported politics, my editor was John F. Bridge, one of the
founding fathers of the *National Observer*. His kindness in
permitting me to follow my own cantankerous course is ap-
preciated. I would also mention William E. Giles, the editor
of the *National Observer*, who permitted Jack Bridge to
permit me to follow my specialized and sometimes unusual
interests. Beyond that, I would mention the *National Observer* itself, in an institutionalized sense. The *National Observer* is a writer's newspaper. It gives its reporters the time
to prepare a story and the space to tell it. Without the time
and without the space, much of the reporting that results in
this book would never have been done.

A great many people have been indulgent. I am especially indebted to the men who work for politicians. These
are the staff people who are mostly faceless and anonymous

but who, in fact, make things go. In the pages that follow, I mention many of them by name; to each of these, my thanks. I am embarrassed to leave out so many others.

A word too for my colleagues, a ragged little band of reporters who live out of suitcases in such improbable places as the Jack Tar Hotel in Lansing and the El Mirador in Sacramento. Covering politics is often a lonely business, with long nights in strange cities and long hours in crowded airplanes. Their good company made those hours a lot shorter.

One of my colleagues is Alan L. Otten of the *Wall Street Journal,* whose political perception is unexcelled. He has permitted me to pick at his brain and at his files; both were packed with solid information.

And finally, a special word for my wife, Peggy, and my two daughters, Greta and Kathie, for whom there have been lonely times too.

JAMES M. PERRY

Washington, D.C.
January, 1968

THE NEW POLITICS

1

INTRODUCTION

THE WIND BLOWING IN FROM THE HARBOR was cold and salty, and it carried with it an unusual, hard-to-identify smell. I finally remembered what it was—glue; old-fashioned, brown, glutinous glue.

The time was September of 1962, and I was in Boston to report the celebrated "Teddy-Eddie" battle for the Democratic nomination for the United States Senate seat once held by John F. Kennedy. Teddy, of course, was Edward Moore Kennedy, the President's big little brother. Eddie was Edward J. McCormack, Jr., a nephew of John W. Mc-Cormack, Speaker of the United States House of Representatives.

But glue?

It wasn't hard to trace. I was standing across the street, in South Boston—"Southie" in song and legend—from the shingled home of the late Edward J. "Knocko" McCormack, young Eddie's father and the Speaker's brother. The smell of glue was coming from that house. I simply followed my nose, noting as I neared the driveway that the place was

1

festooned with crudely made political posters. "Vote for
Edward J. McCormack, Jr., the QUALIFIED candidate,"
one of them, stretched across the entire second floor, read.
Automobiles and trucks and station wagons moved down
the driveway every few minutes. They all had bumper stick-
ers that read: "I back Jack but Teddy's not ready."

I followed my nose up the driveway, stepping aside as
the vehicles moved down it. In the middle of the backyard
I found what I had been looking for—a huge, steaming glue
pot. A skinny, sharp-faced little man was stirring the pungent
brew with a large wooden ladle. Other men ran around the
yard, their arms full of political posters, placards, and signs.
Three or four picnic tables had been set up in a corner of
the yard, where other helpers were gluing the fragile posters
to wooden backing boards. As soon as enough signs were
finished, they were carried off, still steaming, and loaded
into one of the vehicles. The vehicle, usually a panel truck
or an aging station wagon, would then spurt down the driveway and roar away for Malden or Springfield or North
Adams.

"Where's Knocko?" I asked the little man stirring the
glue pot. He merely pointed to a kitchen window. Staring
from it I saw Knocko's round, florid face. I waved a greeting,
and suddenly the face disappeared. "You a reporter?" the
little man asked. I admitted as much. "Knocko ain't talking
to reporters," he said. "Knocko's been put on ice."

And that was the truth of it. Knocko McCormack, a
figure out of Edwin O'Connor's *The Last Hurrah,* had been
told by his own son to avoid newspapermen. No doubt
Knocko was still proud of his boy; at least he and his friends
were working as hard as they knew how for him, and in the
only way they knew. But the boy was embarrassed by his
father.

It was at that point, I suppose, that I first made the not very original observation that the old political order changeth. Anyone with eyes to see could note the difference between Knocko and Eddie. The difference between Eddie and Teddy was more subtle.

Eddie McCormack is slender and articulate. But there's something about him—a curl of the lip, a deliberate wave of the hair. He hasn't quite made it, and a lot of people could sense it. Teddy Kennedy, like his brothers and sisters, was the real thing—a Boston Irishman who had become, God bless him, a Brahmin.

Eddie McCormack never had a chance. His campaign appealed to old loyalties and old times. Even "Southie," the McCormacks' Gibraltar, turned against him and voted for Teddy, a member of a family that had turned away from that kind of ghetto at least a generation earlier.

That was one of the first political stories I covered for the *National Observer*. It is now more than five years later, and John Kennedy is dead (I was with his entourage in Dallas that day) and Teddy Kennedy is in the Senate, a solid but hardly spectacular performer. His brother Bobby is in the Senate too, and everyone says he will be President one day. No one remembers Eddie McCormack.

There have been dozens of other political campaigns since then, and I have covered many of them. All this time, the old order has continued to change, and intelligent and perceptive people, many of them newspapermen, have chronicled the change.

The obvious point has been made a thousand times— that there isn't much future in politics these days for the Knocko McCormacks. In other words, the politicians themselves have changed. A further, and related, point has been made almost as frequently—that the old, big-city organizations, drawing their strength from ethnic blocs, are no longer very effective. In other words, the organizations have changed.

Both points are valid. So much so that people like Daniel J. Boorstin begin talking about pseudoevents and pseudocandidates and suggesting that show biz has taken over in American politics. Politics, these people say, is becoming an exercise in press agentry. If one looks in the right places—to Ronald Reagan and George Murphy and Shirley Temple and even perhaps John Lindsay—the show-biz argument seems sound enough.

But I don't think so. Beginning perhaps three years ago, I began wondering about an area that few people think or write about—the changing *techniques* of American politics, especially at the campaigning level. The truth from my observations is this: It's not show biz that's taking over in politics; it's industrial and business technology.

This new technology, which is changing the way all of us live, is finally being applied to the most disorganized and unsystematic endeavor in American life—politics. Things will never be the same again.

The new technology is already at work in politics, though most people, politicians among them, have chosen to overlook it. The technique of this book will be to examine this new technology, case by case. We will move along in easy steps, starting with the most obvious examples, working up to some of the most sophisticated.

The first chapter will deal with the political-management firm, as generally represented by Spencer-Roberts & Associates of California. This firm made its initial impact by managing Nelson Rockefeller's presidential primary campaign in California in 1964. It achieved its greatest success in 1966 when it guided Ronald Reagan into the governorship of California.

We shall then examine the work of Joseph Napolitan, another professional campaign manager, in the Pennsylvania primary election in 1966. Napolitan took an almost unknown businessman, Milton Shapp, as a client, and won the Democratic nomination for governor. The significant point is the way in which they defeated—routed—the Democratic organization in Pennsylvania.

Next will be an examination of the polling techniques used by the George Romney organization in Michigan in 1966. Polling, to be sure, is hardly a political innovation. Elmo Roper was taking political polls more than thirty years ago. But the Romney organization uses polls in a way no one else has ever used them. It represents a political and technological breakthrough.

Television is hardly new as a campaign technique either. But, along with all the others, it is now being used in advanced and striking ways. No one has ever used television with such brilliance as Nelson Rockefeller in 1966. We shall analyze that prodigious effort.

Nelson Rockefeller's brother, Winthrop, the governor of Arkansas, has been innovating too. His specialty is electronic data processing, one of the most significant of all the new techniques. We shall see what he has done with his own $7,000-a-month computer, and point out what others are doing. More important, we shall consider the untapped possibilities in this area.

Finally, we'll examine John Lindsay's $2,500,000 campaign for mayor of New York City in 1965. For all that money and for all the hard work, we'll suggest that Lindsay's campaign was in fact an anachronism. We shall point out how that campaign might have been run, and argue that Lindsay could have won by a near-landslide.

There are no doubt other examples of the new politics at work that we might have included in this book. But I think these are the most relevant examples and that, taken together, they best describe what is happening.

Perforce, the approach is piecemeal. That's simply because no one has yet put together a political campaign successfully employing *all* the new techniques. At a state level, I'm not sure anyone ever will. One problem is money; a great deal of it is required to do all these things. Another is manpower. Still another is the question of relevance; some techniques are admirably suited to one situation, not so suited to others.

But someday, I believe, a presidential campaign will be organized in which all these refinements will be brought into play. What kind of campaign would that be?

The candidate's travels (along with the travels of the candidate for Vice-President and a number of other leading party figures) will be scheduled by a computer. The campaign will be laid out by the critical-path method. Polls will be taken over and over and analyzed and cross-analyzed. Spot commercials will be prepared weeks in advance of the election, and their impact will be almost subliminal. Researchers will read the polls and study the data from a "simulator"; the issues they develop will all be relevant, and they will be aimed like rifle shots at the most receptive audiences. Researchers will systematically investigate the opposing candidate, and the new techniques will be used to destroy his credibility. When the election is over, and the candiate is victorious, the pollers will go back to work to see what they did well and what they did badly.

And the candidate? He will be out front, moving from state to state with robot-like precision, being fed the data from the polls and the simulator. He will no doubt be articulate, and probably he will be handsome and vigorous. And he may or may not be qualified to be President of the United States.

2

THE RISE OF THE PROFESSIONAL POLITICAL MANAGERS: FROM CALIFORNIA TO NEW HAMPSHIRE

THERE ARE TWO ESSENTIAL INGREDIENTS of the new politics. One is that appeals should be made directly to the voters through the mass media. The other is that the techniques used to make these appeals—polling, computers, television, direct mail—should be sophisticated and scientific.

How new is the new politics?

Broadly speaking, not so very new after all. The new politics was born more than thirty years ago in, appropriately enough, California. The founders were the late Clem Whitaker and his wife, Leone Baxter (who was still active in 1967); together, they organized the first modern political-management firm, and some of the work they did many years ago is, in some ways, superior to anything being done today.

It is important to note that Whitaker & Baxter was a professional *firm* of political managers. That, in its time, was new. There is, of course, nothing new about political managers as such. Campaigns traditionally have been managed by someone. Some one: The emphasis is individual. This someone was usually an old friend or associate of the candidate. These managers go all the way back to Mark Hanna, McKinley's guiding genius. Later, some of these individual managers took on a tinge of professionalism. FDR had Jim Farley. Nixon had Murray Chotiner.

But Whitaker & Baxter was a company, and its business was managing political campaigns for corporate profit. That was a new kind of politics. And Whitaker & Baxter met at least one requirement of the new politics: The firm appealed directly to the voters through the mass media. It failed to meet the other requirement—heavy reliance on myriad scientific techniques—largely because those techniques had not then been refined.

We shall examine in some detail the work of Whitaker & Baxter because, first of all, it is a useful and relevant introduction to everything we'll be talking about. And, second, simply because the firm's work is interesting. We shall then move on to describe the very recent growth of other political-management firms, concluding with a description of the efforts being made at this writing by one of them to win the New Hampshire presidential primary for George Romney.

Clem Whitaker, son of a Baptist minister, was always something of a prodigy. He began work as a newspaper reporter when he was thirteen. At seventeen, he was covering the state legislature for the Sacramento *Union;* two years later, he was the *Union*'s city editor. He moved on from there to establish, in 1920, the Capitol News Bureau, a press service for eighty small-town dailies and weeklies. He operated the news bureau for the next nine years, making an extra dollar or two from time to time as a lobbyist.

It was about this time that another California newspaperman, Charles Michelson, took over as the Democratic National Committee's first full-time public-relations expert. Hoover was in the White House, and the nation was deep in the Great Depression. Michelson quickly showed what an enterprising public-relations campaign could do nationally; what it did do was to discredit an entire political party. For it was the versatile Michelson who coined the word "Hoovervilles" to describe the tarpaper shacks that thousands of unemployed called home. The Depression, in Michelson's vocabulary, was the "Hoover panic." Public relations smoothly paved the way for Franklin Roosevelt.

California was especially ripe for the same kind of public-relations genius. It was a state almost without party discipline or party structure, thanks largely to what Hiram Johnson and his fellow Progressives thought were "reforms" that would purify California for all time. A confused Woodrow Wilson, touring California in 1911, remarked: "I can't, for the life of me, be certain that I can tell a Democrat from a Republican in this place." Nor could anyone else.

It was during the Hiram Johnson era that laws were passed forbidding parties to endorse candidates in primary elections; forcing all candidates, below the level of the state legislature, to run as nonpartisans; establishing procedures for initiative and referendum. And cross-filing in primary elections, a catastrophic Johnson reform, wasn't revoked until 1959.

It was in 1933 that Whitaker and Leone Baxter (she was then manager of the Chamber of Commerce in Redding, California) first joined forces. The task at hand was the passage of the referendum for the Central Valley Project Act.

The chambers of commerce were for the project, and so were a number of highly placed political leaders. Whitaker and Baxter were hired to ensure passage. In the face of vigorous opposition by the powerful Pacific Gas & Electric Company, the referendum was approved by a comfortable margin.

With that accomplished, Whitaker and Baxter formally organized themselves as Campaigns, Inc. The next year, 1934, they worked to defeat the Democratic candidate for governor, muckraker-Socialist Upton Sinclair. To discredit Sinclair, whose only friends seemed to be the poor, Whitaker and Baxter prepared a series of thirty devastating cartoons. The cartoons were plastered on billboards and inserted in almost every newspaper in California. A typical cartoon showed a blissful bride and groom emerging from a church. Underneath, in large letters, was a Sinclair comment that in a capitalistic society the institution of marriage has the qualities of "marriage plus prostitution." Sinclair was easily defeated.

In their glory days, from 1933 through 1955, Whitaker and Baxter (who institutionalized their partnership by marriage in 1938) managed seventy-five political campaigns in California and won seventy of them.

Whitaker, a tall, thin, weathered man, loved to talk politics. He left some gems. "Most every American loves a contest," he once said. "He likes a good, hot battle, with no punches pulled. . . . So you can interest him if you put on a fight! . . . Then, too, almost every American likes to be entertained. He likes the movies; he likes mysteries. . . . So, if you can't fight, put on a show." Another vintage quote: "It was Patrick Henry who said, 'Give me liberty or give me death!' That's what we call laying it on with a ladle. . . . Even in these modern times, that is the kind of dynamic sloganeering that molds public opinion and wins campaigns."

Critics deplored Whitaker and Baxter's methods. One of them wrote: "The sad fact is that their manufacture of slogans and wielding of ladles has led to a grievous debasement of political debate. . . . Whitaker and Baxter's peculiar contribution, however, has been to make a precise art of oversimplification, to systematize emotional appeals, to merchandise the images they create through a relentless exploitation of every means of mass communication. Compared to these virtuosos, the old-time politician seems like an amateur."

Quite so. But the point is that in California there was no "old-time politician," at least not in the sense that the East understands the term. With no political organization, no party discipline, no widespread party identification, Whitaker and Baxter moved in to fill *all* the vacuums. Using mass media in a highly sophisticated way, they took their clients' messages directly to the voters.

They were guilty of sloganeering, of vast oversimplification of the issues—issues that they determined beforehand. But their techniques were valid; they could have been used by anyone; they could now be used by anyone. The techniques developed to such a fine art by Whitaker and Baxter don't require raw sloganeering or even vast oversimplification. They were the first to find the way to the voter in the absence of the party machine. The approach is especially valid today because viable party machines are now rare exceptions.

What were Whitaker and Baxter's techniques? How did they employ them?

A successful campaign, they once said, requires the best candidate, the best cause, the best plan of action, and the best force of volunteers. Once again, oversimplification; Whitaker and Baxter couldn't discuss their own business without falling into their own professional trap.

A Whitaker & Baxter campaign was a prodigious effort. First of all, overworked assistants (the staff, from an off-season low of sixteen, would expand to as many as eighty during a campaign) compiled complete dossiers on their own candidate and on the opposition. A single dossier sometimes ran to as many as 1,000,000 words. (One can imagine how grateful Clem Whitaker would be to today's computers.) From this immense amount of material, the assistants extracted reasonably concise summaries for the personal attention of Whitaker and Baxter. Then, in an almost metaphysical kind of drama, the two partners—summaries in hand—retreated into total seclusion. No one, for any reason, was allowed to disturb them. Locked up together, they worked out a master plan for the campaign. They looked first of all for a theme, and they usually came up with one. The theme, they always said, had to be straight, simple, and devastating. It must, they liked to say, have more "corn than caviar."

That completed, they emerged from seclusion and began hammering away at all the details—preparation of speakers' manuals, layouts for billboards, radio scripts, design of postcards, campaign buttons, newspaper ads. And everything revolved around the theme that had been preselected.

In a campaign in 1948, Whitaker & Baxter distributed 10,000,000 pamphlets and leaflets, 4,500,000 postcards, 50,-000 letters to important individuals; it placed 70,000 inches of display advertising (through its own advertising agency), contracted for 3,000 radio spots and twelve 15-minute radio programs. It put up 1,000 highway billboards and 20,000 smaller posters; it prepared slides and trailers for showing in 160 theatres. The campaign was no more than average Whitaker & Baxter. And, of course, successful.

Whitaker and Baxter had supreme confidence in their abilities. Some might have called it supreme ego. Either way, they always insisted upon running their own show. They developed the issues; they created and placed the advertising; they wrote the scripts. It was the candidate's responsibility to pay for what Whitaker and Baxter decided was best. They made their point with clarity, as in this memorandum to local chairmen in Goodwin Knight's gubernatorial campaign in 1954:

The Campaign will concentrate on a few major issues which will be outlined in the Campaign literature, in the Speakers Manual and throughout the Campaign materials. [Whitaker and Baxter favored lots of capital letters, capital words, and italics.] With such a brief working period as that which lies ahead, you will recognize that we must *stick closely to the main issues outlined,* and leave out many of the secondary and less important issues, however interesting they may be to some of us.

There was a certain inherent arrogance, which the two partners tried not at all to cover over. When they first entered the business, Whitaker once said that political campaigns "were the natural province of broken-down politicians and alcoholic camp followers." They also deplored regular party organization and precinct structure. Ineffective and far too expensive, they argued. Presumably it was upon these premises that they felt their efforts should be employed by a candidate.

A regular part of their operation was sophisticated pressure on the mass media in California. In 1936 they established the California Feature Service, through which they distributed a weekly collection of editorials and other material aimed primarily at California's exceptionally large market of small daily newspapers and prospering weeklies. In his illuminating book, *Professional Public Relations and Political Power*, Stanley Kelley, Jr., says that the staff of one newspaper played a game called "Where's the Plug?" each time the California Feature Service's bundle arrived in the newsroom.

Kelley goes on to list a typical example of Whitaker & Baxter material, an editorial entitled "The Farm Bureau Aids CARE":

"California farmers," the editorial began, "under the leadership of the California Farm Bureau Federation, are currently conducting a unique experiment in international goodwill." The editorial ended with a flourish: "The Farm Bureau is to be congratulated for instituting a program of simple, practical help from individuals to individuals which could well prove to be of more real value than many of the grandiose, tax-supported schemes fathered during the post-war years in Washington."

The Farm Bureau was of course Whitaker & Baxter's client. The back-of-the-hand slap at "grandiose schemes" in Washington no doubt reflected the thinking of leaders of the Farm Bureau. But it also directly reflected Whitaker and Baxter's own thinking. They were conservative, anti-big-government Republicans, and proud of it. Rarely did they agree to work with or for anyone who disagreed with this philosophy.

They did work for Earl Warren when he first ran for governor in 1942, but never again. Perhaps they had in mind Harry Truman's comment: "He [Warren] is really a Democrat, and doesn't know it." Whitaker and Baxter turned up in 1945, however, as managers of a well-financed campaign to defeat Warren's health-insurance program, a program Warren initiated that same year. Whitaker and Baxter's agents personally visited more than 500 newspaper offices. Results: 30 of the 50 newspapers supporting the program backed down, and ultimately the number of papers opposing the program went up from about 100 to 432. The governor's program was defeated.

With this effort behind them, Whitaker and Baxter were hired by the American Medical Association in 1948 to fight President Truman's health-insurance proposals. Working out of Chicago, Whitaker and Baxter and a staff of 40 spent almost $5,000,000 in 3½ years. In 1949 alone, they distributed more than 54,000,000 pieces of anti-Truman propaganda. "It was the greatest grass-roots lobby in history," Whitaker declared. The slogan, "The Voluntary Way Is the American Way," seemed to work, for compulsory health insurance remained a dead letter until Lyndon Johnson finally pushed it through for the elderly in 1965. Clem Whitaker died in 1961, and with his passing the firm lost its genius.* Only the echo of Whitaker's assessment of his own work remains: "We feel that people in our state are better informed, more alive to the issues, are better citizens because of our type of activity."

It is somewhat puzzling that no other comparable management firms were organized during Whitaker & Baxter's heyday. Perhaps the explanation lies in California's singular political situation. Whatever the explanation, it is fact that the rest of the country was titillated by Whitaker & Baxter, but hardly compelled to follow in their footsteps.

Even in California, Whitaker & Baxter stood almost

---

* The firm, however, using standard techniques, continues to try to make up for the loss of Whitaker. In 1966 it helped to manage Robert Griffin's successful Senate campaign in Michigan. Spencer-Roberts was there too, running one of the five key congressional campaigns. (See Chapter Four.)

alone, and when Whitaker died it took time—a year perhaps
—for a new firm to fill the void. That new firm is Spencer-
Roberts & Associates, probably the best known of all the
political-management firms in 1967. In any survey of the
new politics, Whitaker & Baxter is a bench mark. Spencer-
Roberts is another, but neither, as we shall ultimately see,
fully developed the techniques the new politics requires.
Not, at least, by 1967.

With Spencer-Roberts, however, there is surely sufficient ambition. "Someday," William Roberts, one of the
partners, told me, "we'd like to manage a presidential campaign." The other partner, Stuart Spencer, nodded in earnest
affirmation.

They may get their chance, for the firm has achieved
stature and a certain amount of fame.

Spencer and Roberts first gained national recognition
when they managed Nelson Rockefeller's California presidential primary in 1964. Rockefeller, of course, lost but it
was surprisingly close, all things considered. Spencer and
Roberts have worked to put Thomas H. Kuchel into the
United States Senate, and in 1967 they were working for
him again. Once they helped to elect John Rousselot to
Congress; Rousselot went on to become a leader of the John
Birch Society. And, in their greatest single achievement,
Spencer and Roberts managed the successful gubernatorial
campaign of Ronald Reagan, movie actor.

Reagan, a raw political amateur, needed Spencer-Roberts, and he is the first to admit it. "They supplied the know-
how," he told me after his inauguration. "I'd never run for
office again without the help of professional managers like
Spencer and Roberts."

Spencer and Roberts are *professionals,* and we shall
examine their work on that basis. However, as we shall

explain, they are not yet complete masters of the new politics. Their work, to date, combines elements of old-fashioned politics and the new methodology. Thus, they are—in effect —a bridge between what has been and what will be.

"We are," says Bill Roberts, "mercenaries."

The firm (it is, in fact, more than just the two men; an important associated partner has been Fred J. Haffner, who worked out of San Francisco through 1967, and the partners employ a handful of talented specialists) is for hire, along with all the expertise the partners bring to it. The sole restriction is that Spencer-Roberts will work only for Republicans. But, as the record shows, almost *any* Republican—Nelson Rockefeller or John Rousselot, Tom Kuchel or Ronald Reagan.

There is no way of knowing what kind of Republicans Roberts and Spencer are; they won't tell, and perhaps they don't care. Their backgrounds offer little insight. Roberts entered politics as the executive director of the Los Angeles Young Republican organization, but that was before the right-wingers infiltrated and ultimately assumed control of the YRs. Roberts graduated to executive director of the Los Angeles County Republican Central Committee, presiding over a staff of twenty-five and an annual budget of $1,000,000. But that too was an administrator's job. Spencer got his first whiff of politics as director of recreation for the City of Alhambra. Later he became a precinct director in Los Angeles with Roberts.

The two men set each other off nicely. Roberts is heavy-set, friendly, outgoing; Spencer is short, stocky, nervous, and a bit short-tempered. Over a period of months, the two men discussed the possibilities of putting together a firm specializing in the management of political campaigns. They took the plunge in early 1960, and became involved in their first major effort later that same year—running Tom Kuchel's primary- and general-election campaigns.

There are a great many differences in the way Spencer-Roberts operates and the way Whitaker and Baxter used to operate. Whitaker and Baxter's cardinal sin, it seems to me, was the way they inverted a relationship that working democracy absolutely requires—the master-servant stance of candidate and political manager. Whitaker and Baxter were masters; the candidates were their servants. They insisted upon such a relationship, and eager candidates could only sign away all their rights and all their responsibilities. Through 1967 at least, Spencer-Roberts has always worked in a servant's capacity. For that much, let us be thankful.

Stu Spencer and Bill Roberts are technocrats; Clem Whitaker and Leone Baxter were propagandists. Political technocracy, which this book is all about, is sexless; it has no soul and a computer for a heart. The candidate, for whom the technocracy works, must supply the human elements. Sometimes he does, which is fine; sometimes he does not, which is frightening.

The technocrats really don't care. Ideology, issues, human emotion—these are not their concern. Ray Bliss, chairman of the Republican National Committee, is almost a caricature of today's technocrat. "Don't ask me about issues," he tells reporters, and then they all repeat together: "I'm a nuts-and-bolts technician." *

So what have the technocrats done lately for political candidates? Let's examine what Stu Spencer and Bill Roberts have done for Nelson Rockefeller and Ronald Reagan—and what they haven't done.

---

* It would be unkind not to differentiate between the technocrat and his work. Ray Bliss, late of an evening, highball in hand, is an interesting and even stimulating companion. Bill Roberts is always the soul of grace. Most of the technocrats, in fact, are exceptionally gregarious, after hours.

The Rockefeller campaign in the California presidential primary in 1964 was Spencer-Roberts's introduction to the big time; it was also the toughest assignment they've ever taken. Almost everything seemed to be against them. Alert observers had long detected a swing in California toward the conservatives. The polls seemed to bear this out: They showed Barry Goldwater leading Rockefeller in the hearts of Californians by 63 percent to 28 percent. In southern California, swarms of young, militant Republicans were marching for Goldwater, delivering, among other things, cartons of conservative tracts like John Stormer's *None Dare Call It Treason* and Phyllis Schlafly's *A Choice Not an Echo* to thousands of approving suburban home-owners. Rockefeller was an immensely wealthy Easterner saying unkind things about a gentleman from Arizona who vacationed every summer down at Newport Beach. Moreover, this man Rockefeller had divorced his wife of many years and married a younger woman who had just been divorced herself. Nasty, nasty, said these people living in a state with one of the highest divorce rates in the world.

But, besides being one of the most successful governors in this century, Nelson Rockefeller is a stubborn man. All that money no doubt helps make him that way. He sent his alter ego, the gracious George Hinman, to California to look the terrain over. Even before John Kennedy was assassinated, Hinman began checking Spencer-Roberts's credentials, and he liked what he discovered. Months later, Hinman, acting for Rockefeller, signed a deal with Spencer-Roberts. Money, of course, was no problem.*

---

* Except in a reverse sort of way. The Rockefeller people didn't want to appear too loaded. Thus, in the last days of the campaign, they cut back on radio and television time. They also cut back on spending for high-visibility items like billboards. As things turned out, it was a mistake.

One of the problems that faces any political-management firm (as opposed to the new political *consulting* firms) is the seasonal nature of the work. It tends to be feast or famine. That means the year-around payroll must be kept to a minimum. Expansion of staff occurs only when the campaign opens and the cash begins to flow. Spencer-Roberts, with all that Rockefeller cash, went through a dazzling period of growth. "The idea," noted Fred Haffner, a Spencer-Roberts partner, "was to go out and hire as many people as possible."

Gross, Roberts, and Rockey, a San Francisco firm specializing in campaign finances, farm problems, and the Negro community, was retained, becoming in effect a part of the Spencer-Roberts organization. Ross Wurm & Associates of Modesto, agricultural specialists, went on the payroll. Agriculture is big business in California, and Wurm and his associates had invaluable contacts in the rich San Joaquin and Sacramento valleys. Wurm put together a paid organization of fieldworkers that ran south to Fresno. The southern anchor man was a raisin grower.

John Wilkes, director of that part of the Rockefeller campaign aimed at the Negro, wrote to every Negro college in America and got the names and addresses of all their graduates living in California. His research showing that the Rockefeller brothers had given more money to these colleges than even the federal government was put to good use.

"We tried to put our dollars to work in new areas—places the party had ignored," Haffner said. There wasn't much choice. In those places the party hadn't ignored, the machinery (such as it was) was in the hands of Goldwater partisans.

Spencer-Roberts succeeded in developing a Rockefeller organization, but almost all of it was a paid organization that lacked the frenzied commitment of the forces working for Goldwater, for nothing. The next job was to bring Rockefeller into the state and let Californians see him for what he is, a friendly, rumpled, serious, hardworking multimultimillionaire. Spencer-Roberts succeeded here too, by developing an absolutely flawless method of turning out crowds.

It worked this way: Given a certain area where the firm wanted to display the candidate, names, usually those of married couples, were drawn from each neighborhood. Formal invitations were then printed. For each of these receptions, Spencer-Roberts managed to find a prominent local Republican to act as host. I attended such a reception at the Thunderbird Hotel at Millbrae, near the San Francisco Airport in San Mateo County, home of some 85,000 registered Republicans. The invitations for that reception read: "Assemblyman and Mrs. Carl A. Britschgi request the pleasure of your company at a reception in honor of Governor Nelson A. Rockefeller." The Britschgis' total contribution was the permission to use their name.

Some 20,000 invitations were mailed to San Mateo Republicans, upon the calculated assumption that 5,000 would turn out. The assumption was entirely accurate; 5,000 came, stood in line, and got a handshake and a mumbled word or two from one of the richest men in the world. "Five thousand got the treatment," Fred Haffner said. "They came from every precinct in the county. They were peeled off from every neighborhood. The word will radiate out to all their friends. We will reach thousands more."

That Rockefeller was reduced almost to incoherent exhaustion was hardly noticed. He stood in the reception line for more than two hours, without a single break, and shook every one of those hands and replied to every halting, irrelevant question and signed every child's autograph book.

After shaking the last hand, he could only mumble, "Oh, boy."

The Millbrae reception was repeated again and again in all parts of California. As I left Millbrae, I heard one of the Spencer-Roberts staffers talking about the next reception in Long Beach. "There are more old people in Long Beach than in heaven," he said. "We'll rack up Goldwater on Social Security there."

The election took place on June 7. By late May, most observers, including this one, thought Rockefeller had gained the lead.* His receptions, after all, had been well attended and enthusiastic. Spencer-Roberts had managed to create an organization of 12,000 "volunteers," each of whom received a weekly newsletter. More than 1,000,000 pieces of Rockefeller campaign literature had been mailed. An immense amount of money had been spent.

But he lost, and Goldwater moved on to the Cow Palace and a first-ballot nomination. Why?

Partly because Spencer-Roberts's performance wasn't all that good. The firm, remember, was just taking on its first big-time assignment. Looking back, there were a great many things that were done badly or not done at all.

"They produced absolutely astounding results in turning out people for our receptions," a Rockefeller aide told me after the election. "We couldn't believe it; we had never seen anything like it in the East."

The crowd gimmick was a good one, given the unusual circumstances. But it was hardly an innovation. A political historian once wrote this about California: Politicians in

---

* The headline on my story in the *National Observer* the week before the election read: "Why Rockefeller Looks like a Winner." My headline the following week was: "How Goldwater Won the Big One in California." There are a number of friends—acquaintances really— who continue to remind me of it.

the old days "used personal contact and individual favors as their basic contact with the electorate. The political management firm depends heavily on the expert use and manipulation of the media of mass communications by professional advertising and public relations men to influence the electorate."

The Spencer-Roberts technique was, in essence, a throwback to other days, despite all its acknowledged refinements. The receptions, it now seems clear, were not enough to get through to the voters in a state in which one of fifty-eight counties alone is as big as Connecticut, Massachusetts, and New Jersey combined.

Spencer-Roberts never developed a master plan; nothing, anyway, comparable to the grand strategy that Whitaker & Baxter always developed. Perhaps it was not their fault, for, as the campaign progressed, more and more Rockefeller advisers streamed into Los Angeles. On a sunny day, most of them could be found basking next to the swimming pool at the Ambassador Hotel. Whitaker & Baxter would never have tolerated such interference. Spencer-Roberts had no choice.

Little things apparently were overlooked. With eight weeks to go to Election Day, no one had remembered to design the highway billboards. Radio scripts weren't written until the final, hectic days when no one knew exactly what to say.

Whitaker & Baxter had always maintained that the voters love a good fight. Spencer-Roberts, or the Rockefeller people, or both, pulled back from what could have been a wildly ferocious fight. The best issue they had against Goldwater was right-wing extremism, then in full, exuberant flower in southern California. A television film, developing just that theme, was prepared, and then at the last minute scrapped. Too antagonistic, someone said. Clem Whitaker would never have understood.

Whitaker & Baxter always contended that every campaign is won or lost in the final three weeks. That claim is debatable (there's a large body of evidence indicating that many elections are decided before campaigning even begins), but it turned out to be fact in California. And it was in the final days of the campaign that the Rockefeller people pulled back; they were ahead, they thought, and they didn't want to rock the boat. At the same time, Goldwater campaigned with more vigor than he had ever shown before or would ever show again.

"Spencer-Roberts's weakness," said a Rockefeller staffer after the election, "is their inability to put together a total campaign and sell it to the voters. They don't understand the mass media. The people of California never came to know Nelson Rockefeller as a person; they never saw the fighting Rockefeller. They failed where Whitaker and Baxter always succeeded, in their ability to sell a candidate."

The criticism is only partly valid. Rockefeller, for all the griping of his staffers, got his money's worth from Spencer-Roberts. No one else could conceivably have done so much. But Spencer-Roberts did learn all kinds of lessons, and it's highly doubtful they'll ever repeat the same mistakes they made in 1964.

The job they did for Ronald Reagan was, given its special requirements, a masterpiece. They did precisely what they set out to do—make Reagan, popular enough with the voters as an actor, acceptable to them as a governor. "If the voters can become comfortable with him, and if any doubts about his ability to do a good job can be erased, then the gates would burst," Stu Spencer told me nine months before Election Day. "School," he added, "would be out." That's what happened; the doubts were erased, and Reagan beat Democratic Governor Edmund G. "Pat" Brown by a million votes.

It was an interesting triumph for Spencer and Roberts; it was almost as if they wanted to show everyone, just for the hell of it, that they could elect a right-wing conservative to high office. And that may have been part of it.

One wonders if Whitaker & Baxter could have handled the Reagan campaign nearly so well. The hardest thing in politics is to keep your mouth shut in the face of overwhelming temptation. Spencer-Roberts decided to play the Reagan candidacy very cool; Reagan never replied, for example, to Pat Brown's early attacks upon his right-wing background or his obvious lack of experience. The advice that Reagan accepted was first rate. In no time at all, Brown was sounding more and more desperate. Always the underdog in the past, Brown began to look like a bully. And Reagan suddenly was, of all things, a statesman.

It is now months after Reagan's inauguration. Important people are talking about him as a presidential candidate. Yet, Governor Reagan still has a curious ring to it. Ronald Reagan as governor?

Spencer and Roberts had the same reaction when a prominent California Republican approached them after the 1964 elections and first raised the idea. "You get a lot of crazy suggestions after an election, particularly after a losing election," a Spencer-Roberts staffer told me. "So we didn't pay a great deal of attention to the idea." But in May of 1965 the firm was approached by Ralph Townsend, a friend of both Reagan and Spencer and Roberts, who indicated that the idea was not so crazy as it sounded. Later that month, the partners met with Reagan and his brother, Neil "Moon" Reagan, a West Coast representative of the Mc-

Cann-Erickson advertising agency, in a Los Angeles "key" club. Spencer and Roberts learned then that they had been recommended to the Reagans by Barry Goldwater himself. Goldwater, it seemed, had been highly impressed by the job Spencer-Roberts had done against him for Rockefeller.

A week later, Spencer, Roberts, and Haffner, the third partner, met again with Reagan, this time at the actor's rambling Pacific Palisades home. That same morning, the three partners had talked to George Christopher, former mayor of San Francisco and ultimately Reagan's opponent in the Republican primary. They also talked to Laughlin E. Waters, a former United States attorney in Los Angeles. Everyone, it seemed, wanted Spencer-Roberts. The partners rejected Christopher and Waters; they accepted Reagan.

A good many people, most of them moderates and liberals, were outraged. Senator Kuchel was especially outraged; he was still debating with himself about running for governor, and he was presuming that Spencer-Roberts would be available to him if his answer turned out to be Yes. "We were shocked, simply paralyzed, when we heard Stu and Bill were going to work for Reagan," a Kuchel ally told me.

Spencer and Roberts saw nothing shocking about it. "For us to work for anyone," Roberts said, "they've got to want us. Kuchel didn't seem to. He never asked us to work for him. We felt from his silence that he wasn't interested in running for governor. After all, we have a staff and an overhead here. We need clients; we'd never been involved in a governor's race, and we wanted to be." *

Except for their imaginative use of computers (which we shall examine in Chapter Six), Spencer and Roberts did

---

* How times have changed! Kuchel was Spencer-Roberts's first major client. He asked Spencer-Roberts to work for him again in 1967–1968. But before the partners said Yes, they asked Reagan if it would be all right. He said it would be, even though his admiration for Kuchel is something less than overwhelming.

not emphasize the new technology in the Reagan campaign. More than anything else, the Reagan campaign was an exercise in gentle restraint. Reagan always led in the polls; the idea was to keep him out there. No show of anger, no show of temper. Nice, cool Ron Reagan.

The original group backing Reagan (and it still is backing him) was fat-cat Goldwaterite. That, decided Spencer and Roberts, wasn't good. Lyndon Johnson, after all, had taken 60 percent of the vote in California. So one of the first things Spencer-Roberts insisted upon was a broadening of the group behind Reagan. Some people who had been associated with the Rockefeller primary campaign were added to the list. At Spencer-Roberts's suggestion, a few Jews were recruited.

Then, by car, by train, and even by airplane (Reagan hadn't flown in years) Spencer and Roberts led their candidate around the state, meeting with political leaders, civic groups, religious organizations. He sat down for hours with men like the publisher of the *California Farmer,* trying to familiarize himself with state issues. He talked to district attorneys and even to cops on the beat. All the while, Spencer and Roberts insisted with straight faces that it was just an "exploratory" expedition to see if the people would find Reagan acceptable as a candidate. Because he hadn't formally announced his candidacy (that came in January of 1966), Reagan was able to talk to nonpartisan groups that might not have welcomed him had he been a live candidate.

Spencer-Roberts continued to display a genius for organization. Reagan committees were created all over the state, and the Spencer-Roberts rule of thumb was that each of them had to include at least one Rockefeller and one Kuchel man. If the committee were especially large, an old Richard Nixon supporter had to be included.

This was a cleverly calculated effort to prove a dubious

point: That Reagan is a mainstream Republican. Look,
Spencer-Roberts seemed to be saying, he can't be a Bircher;
he has all those clean-cut Republicans on his own team. It
was a highly diverting argument.

Spencer-Roberts succeeded in convincing most California
voters that Reagan was responsible, trustworthy, and ideo-
logically acceptable. If not Spencer-Roberts, *someone* toned
down his speeches. They sounded eminently reasonable, although a close reading of the texts indicates Reagan wasn't
changing his very conservative positions that much. His
management was careful, however, in handling the "kook,"
or extremist, points of view. Reagan did not come out
against Social Security (as he had all but done in his in-
credibly inept autobiography, *Where's the Rest of Me?*). He
managed to accept the graduated income tax; he opposed
the Liberty Lobby amendment as unworkable. Spencer-Roberts prepared a careful 700-word statement for Reagan dealing with the John Birch Society. In it, Reagan said that
members of the society ought to reach a decision concerning
"the reckless and imprudent statements of their leader,"
Robert Welch. What that decision should be he didn't say.
Reagan said too that he was not a member of the society
and had no intention of becoming one. He said he was not
seeking support from the society, but nowhere did he say
he would reject Birch support. It was a handy statement:
Whenever the question was raised, he pointed to it as his
definitive position. Copies of it were always available.

Polls measuring voters' attitudes had been taken at the
outset of the campaign. The issues Reagan stressed dove-
tailed nicely with the findings of those polls. Reagan was
against crime; so was almost everyone else. He was for stern
measures to suppress rioting in the ghettos; so, with Watts
fresh in everyone's mind, were most Californians, excepting

poor, frustrated Negroes who were pretty sure to vote for Pat Brown anyway.

Both Spencer and Roberts ordinarily play their cards close to the vest. But in a closed seminar run for Republican politicians by the National Committee in May of 1967, Bill Roberts discussed the campaign in unusually candid terms. From the transcript, here are the highlights of his remarks:

What were some of the public-relations problems we were up against? Well, first, we had a candidate that had no experience for public office whatsoever, against an opponent who had 23 years of public office and eight years as Governor. From the beginning we felt that there was nothing to be gained by trying to compete with him on his own level—that is to say, not trying to become more knowledgeable than he was on a given issue. As an example, by making a long and involved statement on crime and then saying, "Now, Governor Brown, top that." He would have topped it the next day very easily, because he had access to the government research facilities and he would have one-upped us very easily.

So how do you deal with the problem of an inexperienced man against a very experienced one? Instead of trying to be devious or pull maneuvers—and by the way, that kind of approach in politics doesn't go over too well today. The general public is too sophisticated, too well aware, too well educated to fall for baloney very long. And if you think you're going to pull the wool over their eyes, try it. I guarantee your failure 99 times out of 100 today. You've got to come through to them legitimately and solidly because they can sense a phony 20 miles away.

Our answer to that was to be very candid and honest about it and indicate that Governor Reagan was not a professional politician. He was a citizen politician. Therefore, we had an automatic defense. He didn't have to know all the answers. He didn't have to have the experience. A citizen politician's not expected to know all of the answers to all of the issues. It was a foundation point from which, on any issue, he could get as bright as he wanted, but he could always retreat to the fact that he was a citizen politician.

As a matter of fact, before the end of the campaign, he hit it so well and so hard that Governor Brown was on the defensive for being a professional politician.

Frankly, I think it worked out very well. This was the result of the collective thinking of not only the professionals but the candidate himself and his steering committee.

Another problem not quite so serious but still one to be dealt with was the fact that he was an actor. Because he was an actor it was charged that he was just going through the motions and acting out the part of running for governor, with no sincerity. He could memorize a speech, give it, and everyone would say, "That's wonderful, but he is an actor. He memorized the speech and he gave it. He gave it well. But so what? He still doesn't know anything."

So for the most part, during at least the primary and a good portion of the general election, it was mandatory to those groups that we spoke to that a question and answer period follow his speech. This strategy immediately told the audience that he did have a grasp of the issues, that he did understand the important things that were facing the state. Not knowing what the questions would be, they were impressed by the fact that he had knowledge on the subject and was able to deliver it to them. This helped us immensely in killing the point that he was just an actor.

We had to deal with the problem that Governor Reagan was active in the '64 campaign in the Goldwater effort, and proudly so. However, a repetition of a Goldwater type of campaign in California in '66 was not going to be successful. Therefore, the organizational structure was set up with all new people. Nobody who was bloodied and tarred in the '64 race occupied a major front position in the '66 election. Not that they weren't good people. Not that they weren't involved where the public would see them as far as the frontal operations were concerned. We dealt with new young faces to implement our new candidate. I think this was a big factor and helped us immensely in the campaign.

We dealt with the issues that we felt the people were interested in. We arrived at that decision via surveys, via the steering committee's own reaction, and frankly, from the Q and A sessions. The issue concerning Berkeley and the unrest there was not the result of a survey. It was not the result of our own thinking. It was the result of the question and answer sessions after various speaking engagements. Every time, the question came up two or three times. It didn't take too bright a person to decide that we had best join that issue and have a position on it and make a point of it. During the course of the campaign, it became a very strong issue.

So, as things turned out, it was a cakewalk for Reagan. Brown, a good but hardly inspirational governor who had simply gone to the well once too often, was beaten by an incredible one million votes, and a new Republican star was born.

In retrospect, Spencer-Roberts didn't do anything miraculous or even very sinister. There were no special innovations or wild gimmicks. It was not that Spencer and Roberts did anything so positive; it was just that they didn't do anything negative; they never made a major mistake. And that, after all, is a test for most campaigns. The good ones don't make mistakes.

Spencer-Roberts has developed a number of solid assets. Among them:

1. Their political judgment, relating especially to California, is exceptionally sophisticated. They don't rattle easily. They support their own intuition with a careful appraisal of the polls.

2. Their ability to organize at the grass-roots level continues to be without parallel. It's an especially valuable asset in California.

3. They keep their eyes and ears open; they keep learning. Now, for example, they own a piece of a data-processing

firm that is breaking some interesting new ground (see Chapter Six). Too, Spencer-Roberts is finally managing campaigns in other states. In 1966, the firm worked for a Republican congressman in Michigan. That same year Stu Spencer popped up in Wyoming, where he helped to elect a colorless governor, Clifford P. Hansen, to the United States Senate.

Yet, Spencer-Roberts is still weak in a number of areas, all of which importantly involve the new politics. Polling is one. Spencer-Roberts doesn't do its own polling, and the Los Angeles firm it usually hires is not nearly so good as it should be. Spencer and Roberts ought to be taking their own polls; in fact, they were thinking of doing just that in 1967. They still haven't mastered the political uses of television. Through the Ronald Reagan campaign, they continued to assign the production of all their television to advertising agencies. Both Spencer and Roberts admit that the results have been spotty at best. One day, they hope to be able to produce all their own television. As a start, they were producing Tom Kuchel's low-budget television "in-house" in 1967.

Spencer-Roberts's cautious success has not gone unnoticed: In recent years, other political-management firms, some located outside California, have been organized.

One of the most publicized of these firms is headed by Hal Evry of Los Angeles, operating corporately as the Public Relations Center. Evry has a catchy gimmick: Candidates, he says, should never be seen or heard. "Unless the guy is an experienced speaker," Evry told the *Wall Street Journal*, "he's going to do himself far more harm than good getting out there where people can ask him questions."

In his most celebrated success, Evry took in hand a young lawyer named Pat Milligan, and elected him to the board of the San Bernardino Water District. Evry simply came up with a slogan, "Three Cheers for Pat Milligan," smeared it on billboards, ran it in newspaper advertisements, and mailed it to voters. Milligan was elected. Evry, however, is simply a gadfly; he has yet to manage a campaign of consequence. His is a very old game.

Another of the new firms is U.S. R&D, operated by two old Kennedy hands, William Haddad and Robert Clampitt. But, through 1967, they had yet to win a major campaign, and had in fact compiled a staggering record for losses. U.S. R&D worked for the late Robert King High in Florida (he ran for governor and lost to Claude Kirk); Detroit Mayor Jerome P. Cavanagh (he lost the Democratic primary for the United States Senate in Michigan to G. Mennen "Soapy" Williams); and Frank D. O'Connor in New York (who won the party endorsement in convention and then lost the general election for governor to Nelson Rockefeller).

U.S. R&D is one of two major firms that works for Democrats. The other is Joseph Napolitan Associates, whose work we shall examine in detail in Chapter Three.

Another new firm, working only for Republicans, is Campaign Consultants Inc. (CCI), with offices in Boston and Washington, and it may turn out to be the most successful of all the political-management, or consulting, firms.

CCI's president is David B. Goldberg, national director of the Draft [Henry Cabot] Lodge Committee in 1964. Goldberg, then a young Boston lawyer, was chiefly responsible for Lodge's upset victory in the 1964 presidential primary in New Hampshire. Another major figure in the firm is John Deardourff, formerly the research director of the New York Republican State Committee (see Chapter Seven). Deardourff has worked closely with both Nelson Rockefeller and John Lindsay.

Whitaker & Baxter and Spencer-Roberts manage cam-

paigns. CCI has a different pitch: It offers consulting services. It is an important distinction. The brochure announcing CCI's formation stated:

> CCI is a completely new, completely unique service in the
> political field. Its basic method of operation is very similar to
> a well-staffed business consultant firm. CCI has on its own
> staff, or available on a consultant basis from the academic
> world and business, experienced professionals in every phase
> of the political campaign.
>
> Utilized to its fullest, CCI enters the campaign early.
> Its consultants on money-raising lay out a complete plan.
> Experienced organizers divide your campaign area along logi-
> cal lines, working with your people, set up your field organi-
> zation with clear lines of communication and responsibility.
> . . . Above all we are not going to run your campaign. We
> will give you assistance from announcement to victory
> speeches. . . .

CCI's first major client (and this was before Deardourff
joined the firm) was Clayton Gengras, Republican candidate
for governor of Connecticut. It was not a very auspicious
start—Gengras lost to John Dempsey, the incumbent Democratic governor. But the figures were closer than some people
had predicted.

CCI did better in giving advice to two other Republicans. The first was Edward W. Brooke, Republican candidate for the Senate in Massachusetts. CCI told Brooke, a
Negro, to face up squarely to the racial issue, much as John
Kennedy had faced up to the religious issue in 1960. Brooke,
taking that advice, condemned extremists of both the right
and the left. In Maryland, CCI was called in to advise Spiro
T. Agnew, who was running for governor against mugwump
Democrat George Mahoney, whose appeal was plainly racist.

Agnew, taking CCI's advice, turned from a high-level, problem-solving approach to a spirited attack upon his opponent's views. Like Brooke, he won handily.

In 1967 CCI was retained by the New Jersey Republican State Committee to organize a statewide campaign for the state legislature, where all the seats were being contested—80 in the Assembly, 40 in the Senate. The Democrats, prior to the election, controlled both houses.

The Republicans had a problem, and a statewide survey taken by pollster John Bucci measured its dimensions. The poll, taken in late August, showed that 43 percent of the voters expected to vote for a Democratic legislature; 31 percent expected to vote Republican; 14 percent expected to split their tickets, and the rest were undecided. Furthermore, the poll revealed that an overwhelming majority of voters thought Democratic legislators tended to accomplish more than Republicans. And if all that wasn't bad enough, the popularity of Democratic Governor Richard Hughes had climbed back almost to the level it had reached when he was reelected by a landslide in 1965.

There were other findings, and they showed that the voters were worried and unhappy about a number of things —taxes, state spending, the riots in Newark, racial integration, the possibility that Negro children might be bussed to white schools.

So what to do? Bucci, the pollster, urged that the Republicans attack Governor Hughes. He had to be cut down before the Republicans could make gains. CCI, represented by Deardourff and Douglas Bailey, disagreed.

They considered two possibilities. First, they said, the voters' concerns had to be related to what they contended were failings of the Democratic legislature. "We had to link it up," says Deardourff. "Once we made the linkage, we could expect the dissatisfactions to crystallize."

The second possibility was to link these dissatisfactions with President Johnson, whose popularity, as measured in the Bucci poll, was at an ebb. CCI considered this course, and largely dismissed it. It was unreasonable, they decided, to have a candidate for a seat in a state legislature parade around his district attacking the President of the United States. Anyway, they told Webster Todd, Republican state chairman, the President's popularity was too volatile. They had just watched it climb after the summit conference at Glassboro.

The campaign CCI prepared was very simple. They prepared a series of eight large newspaper advertisements, and ran them, one after another, in almost every daily and weekly newspaper in New Jersey. Each advertisement was aimed at a specific, alleged shortcoming, failure, or boondoggle of the Democratic legislature, and each carried the campaign slogan "Vote Republican Before It Gets Worse." Cartoons, drawn by a highly skilled artist, illustrated the advertisements.

There was one other refinement. In the last month of the campaign, Republican Senator Clifford Case and Republican congressmen were brought into the state to attack the Johnson administration. Case, especially, carried the attack effectively.

There were, of course, undercurrents in the campaign that helped the Republicans. The most important of these was a growing feeling on the part of many voters that the Democrats were far too liberal on the civil-rights issue.

Even so, the results were spectacular. Early analyses had indicated that 10 of the Senate seats were safely Democratic,

10 were safely Republican, and 20 were up for grabs. The Republicans held their 10 safe seats, picked up *all* of the 20 swing seats, and even managed to win one of the "safe" Democratic seats. The turnabout in the lower house was almost as dramatic.

Late in December of 1967—as these words are being written—CCI was facing its greatest test. It was organizing George Romney's presidential primary campaign in New Hampshire. Election day was set for March 12, 1968, and almost everyone was expecting that Richard Nixon would be the winner.

Nixon should win; in late December, he was running far ahead of Romney in all the polls being taken in New Hampshire. But CCI was carefully preparing a Romney campaign that would take advantage of many of the techniques of the new politics. The Nixon people were over-confident and they were preparing a very old-fashioned campaign.

Unknown to the Nixon managers, the Romney organizers had opened a computer headquarters in Hanover, and were carefully punch-carding every Republican voter in the state. Fourteen women were at work in that secret headquarters, and by Christmas they had punched IBM cards for 80,000 voters, out of a total of some 148,000. "When we are finished," said a CCI professional, "we'll have the most complete Republican files ever assembled in this state."

Those IBM cards would be used for direct mail to Republican voters. They would enable the Romney people to address personalized, computer-printed letters to, say, all the state's Republican lawyers. Or all the doctors. Or all the members of the Knights of Columbus or the Grange. Romney's message, whatever it might be, was going to get through to the New Hampshire voters with scientific precision. And the Nixon people, at this writing, knew nothing about it.

CCI was simply borrowing a technique developed by Winthrop Rockefeller in Arkansas, which we shall examine in Chapter Six. The Romney polling was being handled by Detroit's Fred Currier, whose work we'll examine in Chapter Four.

CCI was making other plans. Deardourff, for example, was organizing 500 "home" headquarters in every city and village in New Hampshire. Volunteers working out of those headquarters—a refinement developed by the Romney people in Michigan—would canvass voters with computer-printed street lists. They would make phone calls with other computer print-outs. CCI, in late December, already had rented 10 telephone "WATS (Wide-Area Telephone Service) lines" and installed them at the secret Hanover headquarters. It costs $250 a month to rent a WATS line, but you can make unlimited telephone calls with one within the boundaries of an area code—and New Hampshire is all one area code (603). CCI people figured each phone would be used to make at least 200 calls a day for two solid months.

In 1964 Barry Goldwater and Nelson Rockefeller criss-crossed the state day after wintery day, sometimes appearing at meetings attended by no more than a dozen voters. CCI had figured out a technique to overcome that problem—borrowed, of course, from Spencer-Roberts. Just as invitations had been sent out for those Rockefeller receptions in California in 1964, invitations were to be sent out for Romney in New Hampshire. "We'll get two hundred or three hundred people for each meeting this way," said Deardourff.

CCI had hoped to produce a thirty-minute documentary film about Romney's accomplishments to run on television

—borrowing this time from Milton Shapp's primary campaign in Pennsylvania (Chapter Three). But Romney's personal staff procrastinated so long that it wasn't possible to produce such a film.

That was unfortunate; it no doubt would have been effective. Some television, however, was being prepared late in 1967, and CCI personnel said it would be professional and effective.

The Nixon organizers, meanwhile, were assembling a committee that included in its membership every ancient Republican warhorse in New Hampshire. "This," said Stewart Lamprey, president of the New Hampshire Senate and the behind-the-scenes Nixon manager for the primary, "is an organization of party regulars. It is built on a party base and it is the backbone of this campaign for Nixon. These are the proven workhorses from the party's past, and they will be the organization that will run and win this campaign."

The Nixon managers told me it is a mistake for a candidate to appear too often in a New Hampshire presidential primary. The voters get tired and bored. They pointed to 1952, when Eisenhower beat Taft here without ever coming to New Hampshire, and to 1964, when Lodge won the primary, again *in absentia*. Thus, they were recommending that Nixon appear in New Hampshire for no more than seven days (against twenty-two for Romney) and that he deliver a set, formal speech each evening he is in the state.

"I think," said a Romney manager, "that we can win if we run an absolutely flawless campaign, using all the new techniques, and if we get a break. And I am, of course, presuming that Romney is as good a campaigner as we've been told he is."

The stage is set, then, for a major confrontation in New Hampshire between the new politics and the old.* It will be the second such confrontation. The first was in Pennsylvania in 1966, in the Democratic gubernatorial primary. In that one, the new politics triumphed.

*PUBLISHER'S NOTE: As this book went to press, George Romney withdrew from the New Hampshire presidential primary, and therefore the confrontation never took place.

3

A NEW MANAGER AT WORK:
JOSEPH NAPOLITAN
IN PENNSYLVANIA

"I AM A MUCH WISER MAN NOW than I was a year ago,"
Robert P. Casey, a state senator from Pennsylvania's Lack-
awanna County, said. "Politics is changing tremendously.
The old ways no longer work."

Casey ought to know. In the spring of 1966, he was the
official candidate for governor of Pennsylvania's ancient,
crusty Democratic organization. But, on May 17, the Democratic organization was stunned: Mighty Casey was beaten
in his own primary by a stoop-shouldered little millionaire
named Milton Shapp. Never before—not once in history—
had the official Democratic candidate for governor been
beaten in a primary. The organization had always been
master in its own house. And why not? Everyone knows that
in a primary the votes are controlled. In a primary it's mostly
the regulars who turn out—people who are on the state pay-

roll, the beneficiaries of party largesse. The committeemen and the ward leaders make sure they get to the polls. Right? Wrong. Listen to the articulate Mr. Casey:

"You have to do what he [Shapp] did. You have to use the new sophisticated techniques, the polling, the television, the heavy staffing, and the direct mail. You can't rely any more on political organizations. They don't work any more. Patronage? Why, these days, who wants a job in the courthouse or with the highway department? The sons of the courthouse janitors are probably doctors or professional men now. You can't give these jobs away any more. We're at the tag end of an era in Pennsylvania."

And Milton Shapp, a thin little Jew, and Joseph Napolitan, a round little first-generation Italian, supplied the supporting evidence. It was a curious combination—Shapp, the mortally eager candidate, a latter-day Don Quixote, and Napolitan, the jolly campaign manager, a Sancho Panza. But, in their political tilting, they proved their point: that most big-state organizations, especially big-state *Democratic* organizations, have become hollow windmills, endlessly thrashing at turbid air.

So we shall explore in detail the primary battle between Shapp and Casey because it is, to date, the most striking demonstration of what the new technocracy can do when pitted against an unalloyed old-style political organization. We shall (with a touch of guilt) lightly pass over the general election, in which Shapp lost to Republican Raymond P. Shafer, William W. Scranton's self-appointed successor (Scranton, thanks to Pennsylvania's archaic constitution, could not succeed himself). For a number of reasons, the general election was not relevant to the purposes of this book. First, the odds against Shapp were sharply raised because of a national surge in 1966 favoring almost all Republicans. Second, the contrast between the old style and the new was dimmed because the Republicans, led by an effective state chairman, Craig Truax, borrowed a number of pages from the Napolitan effort in the Democratic primary.

First, though, a word about the two central characters, Shapp and Napolitan.

Shapp is one of those big-business mavericks, a millionaire whose political orientation has always favored the Democrats. Starting with just $500 in 1948, Shapp founded the Jerrold Corp., an electronics company that manufactures television antennae and components for community television networks. By 1965, Jerrold employed 2,100 workers in five factories and a research laboratory. But, for Shapp, corporate success was not enough. He has always been entranced by politics and by politicians. In 1960 he paid for full-page advertisements in national newspapers, endorsing, as a businessman, the candidacy of John F. Kennedy. Most people thought it was a ludicrous waste of money. It was also during the 1960 campaign that Shapp cornered Bobby Kennedy in an airplane and urged upon him the idea of proposing a Peace Corps as a campaign issue. How much Shapp's importuning had to do with the acceptance of the proposal is still not clear. But it was typical of the man that he would go to such lengths to get his point across.

Shapp's enchantment with politics reached the point where, in 1963, he decided he'd like to run for the United States Senate seat occupied by that sly and cunning Republican Hugh Scott. He went to Washington to talk it over, and was told to get in touch with Joe Napolitan, who had worked for the Kennedys in the 1960 campaign in a minor capacity. *Life* magazine's Richard B. Stolley tells the story of Shapp's first meeting with Napolitan:

"Milt Shapp introduced himself and said he was interested in running for the Senate. Joe eyed the little, rumpled stranger and asked, 'What state?' Told Pennsylvania, Joe said it would take a great deal of money. 'Do you have any idea how much and where you'll get it?' he asked.

"Shapp quietly explained how he had founded Jerrold and added that, at the moment, his personal net worth was approximately $12,000,000. Napolitan listened in awe. Soon thereafter he began to spend one day a week in Philadelphia to help Milt Shapp put together his campaign for the Senate."

That effort was quietly aborted. There were other prominent Democrats jockeying for the nomination, and most leaders of the organization tended to dismiss Shapp out of hand.* But Shapp, no quitter, plunged deeper into public service and political fervor, neglecting his own business. He hired experts to study Pennsylvania's economy, and issued two background papers called "Shapp Reports." One was about the general condition of the Pennsylvania economy; the other dealt with problems in the steel industry. Each report was mailed to about 50,000 influential Pennsylvanians. The cost to produce them: about $100,000. Any fool could see Shapp was getting set to run for office again.

But what kind of candidate would he make? After all, everyone was saying, a candidate ought to be in the image of John Kennedy—handsome, witty, athletic. John Lindsay escalated the notion. Joe Napolitan, who is something of a flagellant, summed up Shapp's liabilities in a confidential

---

* Napolitan urged Shapp to run, believing he could beat the man ultimately endorsed by the organization—Supreme Court Judge Michael A. Musmanno, a dreary soul whose major claim to fame is his self-appointed role as guardian of the United States flag. Musmanno was beaten by the slimmest of margins in the primary by a "reform" Democrat, Genevieve Blatt, who promptly lost the general election to Senator Scott. "If he [Shapp] had run against Musmanno, he almost surely would be a senator today, because Johnson carried the state by 1,600,000 votes," Napolitan says.

report written after the general election. He made these
points:

> Despite several years of writing about Pennsylvania's
> economic and social problems, and heading the drive to get a
> new constitution for the state, Shapp was not well known to
> the voters when the campaign started.
>
> He is Jewish. I don't think that being Jewish in itself
> cost Shapp the election—but I'm pretty sure it didn't help
> him very much.
>
> He is divorced and remarried.
>
> His physical appearance is not impressive. If Shapp's
> body were proportionately as big as his brain he'd weigh 250
> and stand six-feet-five. [Like Clem Whitaker, Joe Napolitan
> occasionally wields a heavy ladle.] As it is, he is small in stature,
> stoop-shouldered, and when he smiles he wrinkles his nose
> like a rabbit.
>
> Shapp was not the best speaker in the world when the
> campaign began. Or when it ended, for that matter. . . .
> Shapp has a tendency to prolong a sentence instead of making
> a point and cutting it off sharply.
>
> No base of power. Shapp started out with no base of
> power at all, either geographic or organizational. He had a
> small coterie of devoted followers, but no big power bloc.
> [Casey, for example, had Lackawanna County in the primary,
> and his home county delivered him a whopping majority of
> 22,000 over Shapp.]
>
> An unquenchable desire to attack Scranton. Whether the
> acceptance of Scranton as a good governor by the public in
> Pennsylvania is justified or not, the fact remains that the
> feeling exists.
>
> An unfortunate tendency to shoot from the hip.

Balanced against these negatives, Napolitan wrote, were
a number of positives: Shapp is intelligent; he has a creative,
imaginative approach to problems and is willing to try new
ideas; he was willing to spend his own money; he worked
hard; he was willing to listen to advice; he is a decent human

being with a real concern for people.

All very well, and possibly even true. But, in the final analysis, the leading asset was Shapp's money, and his willingness—nay, his eagerness—to divest himself of it. Without all that cash, Napolitan wouldn't have signed on with Shapp —and not just because Napolitan wanted to collect a bundle for himself. Quite the contrary. Napolitan says, and I believe him, that he was paid $10,000 for managing the primary (at the rate of $2,500 a month) and a flat $25,000 for managing the general election. "I had a real incentive in the Shapp campaign," Napolitan says. "I wanted to prove I could beat the organization." To do that, Napolitan needed a lot of money. He got it.

Compared to Milton Shapp, Joe Napolitan is something else. Napolitan is gregarious; Shapp is naturally reserved. Napolitan is earthy; Shapp can pass for an intellectual. Napolitan's idea of a pleasant evening is an all-night poker game. Shapp would rather take his wife to a concert. Both, however, are self-made.

In 1946, when he was seventeen (shades of Clem Whitaker), Napolitan went to work as a reporter for the Springfield, Massachusetts, *Evening Union*. A few years later, after a stint in the army, he went to American International College (AIC) during the day, worked as a sportswriter at night.

It was in 1957 that Napolitan took his first fling at campaign managing. He handled the press and advertising for Thomas J. O'Connor, a Democrat running for mayor in Springfield. O'Connor defeated the incumbent in the primary and went on to win the general election. The next year, Napolitan worked for one of nine Democratic candidates for district attorney. He won the primary again and the succeeding general election. "It was then that I began to realize that how you conduct your campaign has a lot to do about whether you win or lose," says Napolitan. "The Republican in that general election had some good, solid stuff in his background, but he never used it."

In 1959 Napolitan and another Massachusetts Democrat, Lawrence F. O'Brien, joined forces to manage a charter-reform campaign in Springfield. O'Brien, of course, went on to become the presiding political genius for John Kennedy; later, he became postmaster general. In mid-1967, there was still an "O'Brien office" in Napolitan's headquarters in Springfield. But, despite rumors to the contrary, the two men were never partners, and they are not today. In 1960 Napolitan tagged along with O'Brien, working for Kennedy in New Hampshire, Wisconsin, and West Virginia. He then dropped off to manage Endicott Peabody's gubernatorial campaign in Massachusetts. Peabody finished second in a seven-man field in the Democratic primary. It was Napolitan's first loss.

Other political jobs, none of them very notable, followed. Then, in 1962, Napolitan began work as a pollster. He was the pollster, and part-time strategist, in George McGovern's Senate campaign in South Dakota, and he helped to manage Thomas McIntyre's Senate campaign in New Hampshire. He did some polling for Ted Kennedy and, starting late in September of 1962, he went to work for Peabody again. This time, the Harvard All-America football player was elected governor by a slim 5,431 votes. Peabody ran again in 1964, and lost; Napolitan was only peripherally involved. That same year, Napolitan also found time to swing around the country with Larry O'Brien to assess Lyndon Johnson's chances. They found that the President was so far ahead of Goldwater that neither of them could suggest a thing.

By 1965 Napolitan had developed his own ideas about

running political campaigns. "Every month," he says, "I had been learning more about how to win elections. You take a guy who's been a lawyer, a schoolteacher, or a business executive. He keeps working at his own specialty. Well, so had I, and mine was running political campaigns.

"Campaigns are big business today. Each year, they're more expensive. I figure that campaigns for the U.S. Senate and governor in each of the ten biggest states now cost at least $1,000,000 apiece. If you were to invest that much in business, you'd want a consultant. If you were going to spend that much for a building, you'd want an architect. It's the same thing with campaigns. I think every campaign that costs $1,000,000 will be professionally managed within the next ten years. It's just bound to happen."

And so two forces were joined: Milton Shapp, who wanted to be governor of Pennsylvania and who was willing to pay for it, and Joe Napolitan, who wanted to test his campaign theories if only someone would pay the freight.

Napolitan arrived in Philadelphia in January of 1965. He brought no entourage with him, for he had none. Unlike Spencer-Roberts, Napolitan works almost alone. His musty office in Springfield is staffed by a secretary and a woman who tabulates the IBM cards for Napolitan's polls and runs them through a sorting machine. His office in Washington is staffed by a secretary and an experienced public-relations expert.

He and Shapp agreed that the decision to run or not to run would be made by January 1, 1966. Both men were pretty certain the decision would be positive—*unless* former Governor George M. Leader, who was more popular out of office than he had ever been while in, decided he would run. No one, Shapp and Napolitan decided, could beat Leader.

The showdown didn't occur until the night before

Shapp announced his candidacy, late in January. He and Leader met privately at the Locust Club in Philadelphia. "I'm holding a press conference in the morning to announce my candidacy for governor," Shapp reportedly said to Leader. "If you tell me that you are going to run, I'll hold the press conference and announce that I'm not running but that I am supporting your candidacy. But if you tell me that you are not running, I'll announce my candidacy, and then I'll be in the race to stay."

Leader admitted he was under a lot of pressure to run, and he mentioned the possibility that the White House itself might soon be prodding him. But Shapp was ready for that one. He had contacted the White House and received assurances that the President would not intervene. "It won't happen," Shapp said.

Finally, Leader said: "Milt, as of this time I'm not a candidate and my inclination is not to run." The next morning, in Harrisburg, Shapp announced he was a candidate for governor.

There was still the question of whom the Democratic organization would endorse. Shapp was certain he wouldn't be the choice. Earlier, he had called on David Lawrence, a former governor and acknowledged leader of the party in Pennsylvania. When the meeting ended, someone asked Lawrence what advice he had given Shapp. "Nothing," Lawrence said, "except to stay out of the race. It's pitiful to think that a man can get himself worked up to that kind of pitch. His candidacy is such a hopeless thing." *

The Democratic organization in Pennsylvania makes its

---

* Lawrence had only a few months to live. Shocked as he was by Shapp's primary victory, he worked hard for him during the general election. He was speaking for Shapp at a rally just four days before the election when he was stricken by a heart attack. He lingered in a coma for days; he never knew who had won, but he knew he had done his duty for the party.

endorsements through its State Policy Committee, a group of some 120 persons from all sections of the state. Shapp, whose major issue in the primary turned out to be an attack on the "bosses," was himself a member of the Policy Committee, representing Montgomery County, outside Philadelphia.

While Shapp and Napolitan were preparing a campaign that would shortcut the organization and go directly to the voters, young Senator Casey was following historic precedent. He toured the state, talking to all the organization leaders and week after week nailing down a vote in the Policy Committee here, another there.

But Casey was not the choice of the "bosses," not of the big bosses anyway. In Pennsylvania, the big bosses come from the two big cities, Philadelphia and Pittsburgh. Casey never solicited the support of these party leaders. "If there ever was a candidate who wasn't picked by the bosses—whoever they are—it was me. What I did in winning endorsements was to surround the big cities. They finally had to go along with me because I had everyone else.

"But while I was lining up endorsements, he [Shapp] was building a staff and opening headquarters all over the state. When the campaign started, he had an extensive staff. I had nobody. The best I ever managed was to get a campaign manager, hire three men to write press releases and speeches, put a few girls to work as secretaries in our headquarters, and line up a driver to take me around the state."

Bitter as he may be, Casey refuses to fault the old leaders of his party. "Remember this," he says in their defense, "up until then the primary was take-it-easy time in Pennsylvania."

The organization leaders saw no reason why they should do anything else but take it easy against the challenge of little Milton Shapp. One of their mistakes was of the kind that many politicians make: They read more into the polls than the polls really disclosed. A poll detailing voters' preference should never be used to predict how a vote will go in an election weeks or months away. All such a poll does is give a rough indication of how a hypothetical vote would go at the time the poll was taken. The polls in early 1966 showed Casey an easy winner. In January of 1966, as a matter of fact, a Napolitan poll showed that only 5.2 percent of the voters in Pennsylvania had ever heard of Shapp. As late as mid-April, just a month before the primary election, another Napolitan poll showed that only 20.5 percent of the *Democratic* voters had heard of Shapp and that only 6 percent of all Democratic voters had decided to vote for him.

Given that kind of news, most old-style politicians would privately concede the election and start looking for ways to save money. Napolitan especially, and perhaps Shapp partly, remained confident.

One factor to remember: Napolitan had begun work on the campaign in January of 1965, months before Election Day. In all the case histories we shall consider in this book, the winning side had ample time. Time is absolutely essential. No manager, no matter what his skills, can put together a sophisticated campaign using all the refined techniques unless he has time. It's almost as important as money.

At the outset, Napolitan did the things a good campaign manager should do. He took his basic poll to determine voter attitudes. He hired the best television producer he could find. He realistically outlined the problems he would have to overcome. Those problems, he concluded, were these: (1) getting the people to take Shapp seriously; (2) getting Shapp better known; (3) deciding the best course to oppose the organization in the primary.

Napolitan also began slowly to build a staff. He brought in Oscar Jager, a veteran labor "skate," as press secretary and chief speech writer. Bob Kane, former deputy director of the Democratic State Committee, and Michael Malin, a young lawyer, were hired as organizational experts. Unlike Napolitan, both of them had some knowledge of Pennsylvania's geography and demography. But organization, in the traditional sense, never amounted to much. The idea was to win with the mass media, and the Shapp campaign never veered from that approach.

Napolitan is a firm believer in polling, even though, as we shall see later, his polling techniques are not nearly so refined as those used by a number of others. "Polls," Napolitan says, "never won an election. But you can win an election with what you do with your polls." Of all the polls taken during a campaign, the first one—the basic poll—is the most important, because it determines the messages that should be carried to the voters in campaign literature, billboards and signs, and television and radio spots.

A basic poll is expensive because it covers so much ground. Sometimes it takes an interviewer forty-five minutes to complete one interview in such a poll. Thus, the cost runs between $6 and $10 an interview. In a state like Pennsylvania, a basic poll ordinarily costs up to $9,000. Napolitan, in testimony to his own confidence in polling, took *four* statewide polls for Shapp. "Hell," he says, "we poll all the time."

The original basic poll revealed nothing terribly useful. Most voters were content with things; the upturn in the economy had greatly benefited Pennsylvania, whose industry is heavily concentrated in coal and steel. Governor Scranton was generally popular with the public, the first governor of

Pennsylvania in man's memory to survive his four-year term intact.

But there was one possibility: A great many voters were convinced that the Democratic Party was ruled by cigar-chomping, wheeler-dealer "bosses" from Philadelphia and Pittsburgh, two cities that many suburban and rural Pennsylvanians view as reincarnations of Sodom and Gomorrah. Shapp himself came up with the slogan to capitalize upon that sentiment in the primary—"The Man Against the Machine."

Never mind that Shapp would have eagerly accepted that sinister machine's endorsement, had it been available. Never mind, either, that the machine was in fact almost a fiction. And, finally, never mind that young Bob Casey was an honest, attractive, intelligent candidate who didn't think much of rule by machine either. And so the decision was made to send Milton Shapp charging through Pennsylvania on a white horse, lance in hand, to clean up all of his own party's dirty laundry. Politically, it was a sound decision, *for the primary*. It tended to lose its impact in the general election when Shapp and the machine joined hands to fight the Republicans.

The message was probably carried most effectively on television, an area in which Napolitan once more has his own opinions. "Effective use of television," he says, "is the key. Everyone uses television now, but some candidates have yet to realize you can *lose* votes on television. You lose them when you put your guy in front of a camera, the kind, you know, where he starts out, 'Good evening, ladies and gentlemen, my name is Joe Blow and I want to talk to you tonight about taxes.' When you do that you can hear the click of sets being switched or turned off all over the state. That sort of program is just radio with a light to read by."

Napolitan believes in allotting a "substantial part" of the budget to production of television programs and spots. "When some candidates have, say, $100,000 for television, they put maybe $5,000 into production so they can spend more on [air] time. I'd rather spend $30,000 on production and only $70,000 on time. The truth is that you just can't make good, cheap films."

The firm Napolitan hired to produce Shapp's television was Guggenheim Productions, Inc., then of St. Louis. For a total price of about $120,000, Guggenheim produced all the spots and the programs for both radio and television that were used in the primary and general elections.

Two of the Shapp films were half-hour documentaries, one for the primary and another for the general election. By far the most effective was the primary documentary, titled, not surprisingly, "The Man Against the Machine." The film opens with a shot of the statue of Boies Penrose on the grounds of the State Capitol in Harrisburg. The choice was splendid because Penrose, a Philadelphia Brahmin and a Republican, was perhaps the most cynical boss Pennsylvania —which once almost had a corner on political cynicism—ever produced. The announcer's voice (Guggenheim hired a professional narrator, Shelby Storck) ticks off a few Penrose gems:

" 'Politics is a profession,' he [Penrose] once said. 'Better to lose an election than lose control of the party,' " the script reads. It continues:

"The majestic figure of Boies Penrose looks across the street to the professionals of another generation. They are the faces of organized politics in Pennsylvania, February 1966. The waiting press and newsreels have known most of them for many years. They are the veterans of the ward head-quarters and the precincts. They are the hundred or so members of the Democratic Policy Committee, who have permits to pass through the doors that will then close. Inside they will name a candidate for governor. It will take an hour to meet, vote, and adjourn. Admission to members only. Admission is by list. There will be no minutes or records. The meeting will be closed. Press and other Democrats outside."

While Storck (who wrote the script and directed the filming too) narrates these horrors, the camera actually shows the sergeant at arms checking off the names of the "bosses" as they arrive for the Policy Committee's closed-door session. Then the big doors swing closed. Only then does the title of the documentary flash across the screen, "The Man Against the Machine."

"Our primary film," says Napolitan, "was the best thing of its kind ever done." That may well be so. I watched the film, and was duly impressed. Even at thirty minutes' duration, it easily manages to hold the viewer's attention.

Yet, a whole half-hour. Most experts these days shake their heads at the idea. Too long, they argue. What they forget is something political managers should always remember: That what works in one campaign doesn't necessarily work in another. Or vice versa. Every campaign is a new start, with its own singular requirements. A half-hour documentary would hardly have been appropriate for Nelson Rockefeller in 1966; he relied (see Chapter Five) on a series of brilliant spots. But, for Shapp, thirty minutes was fine. No one knew much about him; there was something worth saying, and there was a natural curiosity about him. People who watched the film were impressed, and they told their friends about it. The word spread.

With—and here a diversion—the exception of most newspapermen. These new campaign techniques pose a special problem for political reporters. Most of them still tend to

dog the candidate's footsteps, reporting almost stenographi-
cally what he says in his public appearances. But that's just
a segment of the total campaign, and probably not even the
most important segment. In a mass-media campaign like
Shapp's, the battle is waged in the voters' homes. The voter
reacts to what he sees on television and to the campaign
material he receives in the mail. In the Shapp campaign,
only a relative handful of the voters actually saw the candidate in person. And, probably, not many more read in any
great detail what he said as reported in news stories.

During the primary, Napolitan urged Joe Miller of the
Philadelphia *Inquirer* to take a look at the film. Nobody,
Napolitan suggested, could appreciate Shapp's campaign
without seeing it. "He [Miller] never did," according to
Napolitan. "The day after the primary he wrote an 'inter-
pretive' article telling how Shapp won the election, and
missed the mark by a mile or so."

It should be noted here too that Napolitan and the
Inquirer had a running feud from the beginning to the end
of the campaign. Napolitan insists the *Inquirer*'s coverage
was biased; an outsider, viewing the evidence, must agree.

Newspapermen weren't alone in overlooking the critical
importance of the film. The Democratic "bosses" overlooked
it too. Napolitan says that David Lawrence, supposedly
Pennsylvania's supreme boss, never saw it. "If he had," says
Napolitan, "I am certain he would have realized its effectiveness, and attempted to prod the organization to greater
efforts."

The effect the film had upon the old-style politicians
supporting Shapp (there were a few, most of them "outs"
trying to get even with the "ins") is interesting. As Napolitan tells the story, Charles Guggenheim "flew the film from
the California laboratory to Cleveland one night, rented a

car and drove one hundred miles or so to Erie, where Shapp was making a talk. The plan was for Shapp to see the film in a motel room about midnight. His meeting took longer than intended, and at one o'clock in the morning he called Guggenheim to tell him he simply was too exhausted to go to the motel and see the film. . . .

"Bob Kane was at the motel with a handful of politicians from Erie. They had expressed grave doubts about the effectiveness of any thirty-minute film ('nobody will watch it'), but after waiting a couple of hours for Shapp they decided to watch the film anyway. Kane called me early the next morning to tell me they had been bowled over by the film. The film was played heavily in Erie—and we wound up by winning Erie County by more votes than Casey won Philadelphia."

But it was not only the quality of the film that was so outstanding; it was the clever timing of its showing. The primary election was on May 17. The documentary wasn't shown anywhere in Pennsylvania until May 9. Then it appeared everywhere. On May 16, the night before the election, it ran ten times in Pennsylvania—and twice each in Philadelphia and Pittsburgh. A half-hour of prime time on a television station in Philadelphia costs about $3,500. In all, the film was shown thirty-five times on Pennsylvania television.

"My contribution to the making of that film," Napolitan says, "was finding the best guy in the country to do it, and then staying out of his way and seeing that everyone else stayed out of his way too. Of course I had veto power over the product, but I didn't exercise it. We didn't make a single change." It was, however, at Napolitan's suggestion that the Guggenheim crew filmed the closed-door preliminaries to the State Policy Committee meeting.

Once, advertisements in newspapers were the major item in any campaign budget. Napolitan isn't much impressed by the results these days, however. Almost all the Shapp newspaper advertisements ran on the television pages to promote the television programs, especially the half-hour documentaries. But even that was costly enough. "I would guess," Napolitan says, "that we spent as much to promote the programs as we did for the time it cost to show them." *

It is worth noting here that money alone is no guarantee that the candidate will get prime time for political broadcasts. Radio and television stations are under no mandate to sell time to a political candidate. The candidate gets in line just like anyone else—the deodorant manufacturer or the cigaret-maker—and takes what he can get. There is, of course, a federal requirement that stations make "equal time" available to the contending candidates. Napolitan points out that both the Democrats and the Republicans had trouble getting the time they wanted. During the general election, Napolitan wanted to buy as much prime time as he could in the Philadelphia market to show his half-hour documentary. He was able to buy only two prime-time slots. And one station, KYW, wouldn't make any prime time available at all; the best offer was a slot between 1:00 and 1:30 A.M., "hardly," as Napolitan notes, "an hour to catch many viewers." Because of these difficulties, one of the unsung heroes of any successful campaign is the worker assigned to time-buying.

Napolitan, in listing his campaign priorities, puts television first. His second choice divides almost evenly between radio and, of all things, direct mail.

------

* Napolitan is a bit testy about newspapers that are always harping in their news and editorial columns about the rising costs of political campaigns. Often, he says, these same newspapers hike their rates for political ads far above what they charge their other customers. Sometimes "the political rate is double the regular advertising rate, with no discounts allowed, and cash on the barrelhead. . . ."

Radio is obvious enough. It doesn't cost a great deal of money; it's easy to produce (sometimes, the audio from television can be used almost without change). The major challenge is a good, clear script and a good voice. During the primary, the actor David Wayne recorded the Shapp spots; in the general election, Ed Binns, another actor who has become a regular at this sort of thing, took over. For what it's worth, Napolitan thinks Wayne did the better job.

Direct mail, however, seems positively old-fashioned. Most of us have been getting sleazy political broadsides in the mail for years; a lot of people no doubt throw them out without a glance, just as if they were junk mail from any other source. Napolitan and most progressive campaign managers believe, however, that *good* direct mail can achieve impressive results. One significant point is the increasing mobility of the population. Person-to-person contact, once so important, is receding. Whole blocks in many subdivisions are without any recognized group leader. Direct mail, in that kind of situation, fills a necessary communications gap.

In the primary, the major piece of direct mail was a sixteen-page brochure that Napolitan hoped to mail to every Democratic household in Pennsylvania. He fell short of that goal, but still managed to distribute 1,000,000 brochures. The title of the brochure once again was "The Man Against the Machine." Following the lesson imparted by Clem Whitaker so many years ago, all the Shapp campaign materials were tied into that central theme.

Volunteers were used in the primary to address and to mail the brochures. Even so, it was a costly business. Each label costs a half cent. Then there are the expenses of renting the machinery, paying the machine operators, and transporting and processing the bundles. Each primary brochure cost three cents to produce, $2\frac{7}{8}$ cents to mail, and a half cent to process. Total cost was about $65,000.

In the general election, Napolitan decided to employ a commercial mailing house. Surprisingly, that operation turned out to be cheaper, if not much more efficient. The general-election brochure, again running to sixteen pages and titled "Milton Shapp Makes Sense for Pennsylvania," was supposed to go to every household in Pennsylvania. Napolitan suspects, however, that delivery was spotty. The printing of this brochure cost $120,000; postage amounted to another $100,000, and processing worked out to $32,000 (which, as Napolitan notes, was about a penny for each of the brochures, covering label addressing, bundling, marking as third-class mail, and delivery to the post office or pickup point).

In direct mail, as in everything else, plenty of time is an absolute necessity. For that general-election brochure, Napolitan ordered the paper in June. Copy and photographs were prepared in July and early August. Copy approval and design layout were completed in August, and mechanicals were ready for press at the end of the first week in September.

The sheer volume of material poses problems too. "The mailing house could handle only about half-a-million copies a week, and as we had envisioned a mailing of approximately 3,500,000, this meant it would take seven weeks to complete the addressing. The books started rolling off the presses the second week in September, and the first ones went into the mail around October 15. We actually mailed about 3,200,000 brochures." *

There were other pieces of campaign literature, especially in the general election, some produced for direct mail, others ordered just for distribution by hand. A number of

---

* There's an easier way to handle some kinds of direct mail—by using computers. That will be examined in Chapter Six.

these pieces fall into the category of "clientele literature," that is, material aimed at a specific audience. Ordinarily, though, Napolitan doesn't care to aim specific material at ethnic groups; this, of course, is a time-honored campaign device. "I just don't believe in ethnic appeals," he says. "They don't work. There are 6,000,000 people in Pennsylvania eligible to vote. In an interesting election, maybe 5,000,000 of them will vote. You can't divide them up ethnically, except perhaps there's a breaking-up point on whites and Negroes. If I had the choice between a mailing on 'Free the Captive Nations' and one on 'Hold the Consumer-Price Line,' you can bet I'd take the one on prices."

But in every campaign the pressure from special-interest groups is intense. Sometimes, if there's money aplenty, the easiest and most politic way is to give in. So it was that in the general election Napolitan produced a veritable flood of campaign literature. To show just how wide the range can be, here's a rundown of the material produced for the general election:

1. The sixteen-page "Shapp Makes Sense" mailer. This came in five regional editions, with one page changed to emphasize a local issue or condition.

2. A booklet called "Something Wonderful Is Happening in Pennsylvania," which stated no such thing. The quotation was taken from Ray Shafer, the Republican candidate; the booklet showed everything that was *wrong* with Pennsylvania, from water pollution to poverty. Hugh Scott called it "political pornography," and a number of newspapers attacked it. Napolitan concedes that "we may have been hurt by the effect of these charges on voters *who did not see the piece.*"

3. Two four-page brochures produced in comic-book

style. One dealt with automobile insurance, the other with consumer protection.

4. A brochure documenting the alleged antilabor record of Ray Shafer.

5. A piece aimed especially at Negroes, pointing up Shapp's record on civil rights.

6. A four-page brochure explaining Shapp's position on taxes he thought the public utilities should be paying.

7. A small foldover general-purpose brochure that was widely distributed at rallies and other campaign events.

8. A "Compare the Candidates" leaflet in which Shapp was an easy winner.

9. A leaflet, "Democrat or Republican—Is There Any Difference?" aimed specifically at hard-core Democrats.

10. Several small one-fold brochures dealing with consumer protection, the elderly, veterans, free higher education, automobile insurance, and the proposed merger of the Pennsylvania and New York Central railroads.

11. A series of foreign-language leaflets in Italian, Spanish, Croatian, Greek, Hungarian, and Polish. The message was general.

12. A giant postcard depicting Shapp talking to a voter. It invited all voters to write to Shapp and list their complaints.

Even that wasn't the end of it. Another brochure described Shapp's programs on one side, and listed the names of Democratic candidates on the other. Each legislative candidate got 5,000 of these, free of charge. High-school football schedules were produced for each of Pennsylvania's sixty-seven counties. Shapp's name and the names of all the Democratic county candidates were listed on the reverse side. Then there were the usual position papers, mailed out only when requested by highly motivated voters.

Napolitan is not convinced any of this specialized material did a great deal of good. "These were good brochures," he says, "if people read them." But the Shapp organization made no unusual effort to see that any of the materials were properly distributed. "Distribution is always a problem, and while we didn't have much left over, neither am I certain that everything got into the intended hands."

Napolitan's instincts, I suspect, are justified. Ordinarily, this kind of outpouring of specialized campaign literature serves essentially a negative purpose—the appeasement of a handful of special-interest leaders who are already committed to the candidate. Yet, a demurrer: If the material is exceptionally good (Shapp's was not) and if the campaign organization takes great care in seeing that the right people get it, and plenty of it, then the results may be positive. The Nelson Rockefeller experience (Chapter Five) would seem to bear this out.

But enough. Clientele literature did not win the Pennsylvania primary. That campaign was won by television, radio, and mass general mailing. There was a theme—Shapp against the sinister Democratic machine—and everything revolved around that theme. The opposition was complacent and lazy.

It seems so simple now. But the results as they came in on the night of May 17, 1966, were stunning. The final figures: Shapp, 543,057; Casey, 493,886.

One of those watching the figures come in that night was *Life* magazine's Dick Stolley. He had written a story delineating the Shapp-Napolitan strategy that had been scheduled for the May 6 issue. But the editors killed the story after checking traditional sources in Pennsylvania and concluding from them that Shapp had no chance at all. At 3:00 A.M., when the Shapp victory was confirmed, Stolley wired his editors: "SHAPP WON." His revised story subsequently ran in *Life*'s May 27 issue. He deserves credit for being the first journalist to sense what was afoot in Pennsylvania.

It was a smashing victory. "I wanted to prove I could beat the organization," Joe Napolitan had said. And he proved it, to his own and every sensible man's satisfaction. Given the new political techniques on one hand and old-style political organization on the other, there's simply no contest.

But, alas, the primary campaign was far from perfect. Shapp and Napolitan made a number of egregious blunders, the import of which didn't become clear until after the primary was over. Those mistakes came back to haunt Shapp and Napolitan in the general election, when they were arrayed against a tough, smart, and aggressive Republican organization.

Because the mistakes were avoidable, they are instructive. Napolitan himself would be the first to agree to that. Once again, he learned another series of political lessons the hard way.

Lesson No. 1: Don't ever pay large amounts to people you haven't carefully investigated.

An added starter in the Democratic primary was Harvey Johnston, a real-estate dealer from McKees Rock, Pennsylvania. He had run in the 1962 primary too, and drawn 162,000 votes. In 1964 he had been chairman of Democrats for Goldwater. He was also at the time of the 1966 primary president of an organization called the National Association for the Advancement of White People.

Shapp, who insists he knew nothing of this background, met privately with Johnston just hours before the deadline for candidates to withdraw from the primary. Shapp asked Johnston to withdraw from the race on the grounds that the organization could be beaten only in a clean two-man race. If Johnston withdrew, promised Shapp, he could have a job with the Shapp organization concentrating in two areas that Johnston supposedly had talked about in the past —highway safety and conservation. Johnston did withdraw; ultimately, he was paid a total of $15,000 by check. Shapp's defenders argue this was for services performed; Republicans, as soon as they learned about it, naturally charged it was a payoff.

It really doesn't make much difference one way or another. What does matter is that the arrangement was shoddy, and it gave the Republicans a wedge wide enough to drive an elephant through. The opportunity was not missed. The Republicans bought time on the two Negro radio stations in Philadelphia and began running spots on August 12, charging Shapp with dealing with a white racist; the spots ran right up to election day. The Republicans also distributed literature pointing up the incident in Negro neighborhoods. Napolitan says that some of this literature came close to calling Shapp himself a racist. The Philadelphia *Inquirer,* no friend of Milton Shapp, ran a three-part series detailing Johnston's connections with Shapp. Napolitan says the *Inquirer* neglected to point out that Johnston had worked for Bill Scranton in his 1962 election, and barely noted that Shapp had repeatedly repudiated Johnston after the facts about his background became known. There was nothing Shapp or Napolitan could do, except to hope that the Republicans would bungle their chance. And of course they didn't.

General-election returns show that Shapp fared poorly in Negro wards. He had expected to carry many of them by 4 to 1 or even 5 to 1. The margin was often cut to a bare 2 to 1. Some of the falloff was undoubtedly attributable to the Harvey Johnston incident. And it's hardly necessary to add that many white voters, repelled by the incident, voted Republican in protest.

Lesson No. 2: Check the credentials of your employees carefully, and never, never let them make unilateral deals with anyone.

One of the employees at Shapp's Philadelphia headquarters was Randolph Holmes, a $75-a-week messenger who claimed to have close ties with a number of prominent Negro athletes. He did manage to bring three great Negro athletes, basketball star Wilt Chamberlain, football star Timmy Brown, and Olympic sprinter Ira Davis to Shapp headquarters to endorse Shapp and have their pictures taken with him. But, as things turned out, their appearance wasn't voluntary; Holmes, or someone, had told them they would be paid for their services. Shapp's defense is that the athletes had come to his office in good faith and he had no choice but to keep a promise, even though it was made by someone who was not authorized to make any kind of commitment. The athletes were paid a total of $1,500.

All these facts were brought out in court hearings held after the Republicans filed a suit demanding an audit of Shapp's primary campaign expenses. Those same hearings turned up other damaging evidence—that Negro ministers had been paid to work for Shapp and to deliver sermons from their pulpits in his behalf. One of these ministers, the Reverend James Hamlin, received $1,038.50. "I never discussed no special salary," he testified.*

---

* Shapp did manage to avoid one trap. A Negro newspaper, according to Napolitan, asked Shapp for $40,000, in return for which it would support him in the primary. Napolitan turned the paper down. Thereafter, he says, "the paper ran some of the most scurrilous cartoons and comments I've ever seen—[and] they were right back in the general election, looking for money to influence their news columns as well as for advertising."

There were other mistakes. Following the primary, Shapp announced he would be willing to coordinate the campaigns of all 281 Democratic candidates for statewide office, Congress, State Senate, and General Assembly—if he was permitted to name his own state chairman. Party leaders refused to buy the proposal. They easily elected their own candidate for chairman, Thomas Z. Minehart, over Shapp's Bob Kane. Shapp then announced, within minutes after his defeat, that he would work with Minehart as best he could. Napolitan, looking back on that moment, suggests Shapp should have walked out of the meeting after his defeat, declaring he would run his own campaign but still operate within the party. In that way, says Napolitan, he would have preserved his image as a fighting independent. Napolitan's right; that's what Shapp should have done, or at least something very much like it.

Then, too, there was the question of Shapp's money, and the way he was spending it. Shapp reported the expenditure of $1,390,000 in the primary; Casey spent only about $250,000. The Republicans, facing no primary battle, spent practically nothing.

The Republican court suit charging that "Shapp and his minions have not filed a full, true, detailed account" was a smart, if phony stratagem. Shapp's accounting of expenditures was improbably accurate (so much so that Napolitan lists honesty of reporting as one of the campaign errors). The court suit emphasized to the general public that Shapp was a big spender. But worse, the testimony seemed to indicate that Shapp didn't really care how he spent his money. No candidate should ever appear too eager, although most of them are desperately so; Shapp emerged from the primary and those hearings as one of the most desperately eager men ever to seek high office.

The Republicans systematically executed an almost classic example of that ancient courtroom tactic—destroying the witness's credibility. First, they attacked Shapp's story about helping to father John Kennedy's Peace Corps. Then they charged he was trying to "buy" the election. The Harvey Johnston incident and the money paid to the Negro ministers and athletes fitted in with that nicely. Finally, they belittled Shapp's issues, especially his program for free higher education.

Giving full credit to the Republicans for inventiveness, Napolitan concluded that theirs was a campaign of "pure character assassination, aided and abetted by the Philadelphia *Inquirer*." The Republican campaign was, to be sure, an aggressive one, but it was not atypical for Pennsylvania. Politics in the Keystone State is tough, and maybe Joe Napolitan, a Massachusetts boy who should have known better, wasn't quite prepared for it.

Anyway, Shapp didn't do *badly* in the general election. As Napolitan notes, Republicans won twelve of the thirteen races for governor and United States Senate in the ten largest states. (Governor John Connally of Texas was the lone Democratic winner.) With that one exception, Napolitan argues, "Shapp ran better than any other Democratic candidate for senator or governor. In addition, he was the only Democrat to improve on his party's performance compared with the last off-year election."

The final vote was: Shafer, 2,110,349; Shapp, 1,868,719.

By Napolitan's reckoning, Shapp spent $2,500,000 of his own money. Or rather, Joe Napolitan spent it for him.

Napolitan says it is unlikely he will ever again be quite so deeply involved in a political campaign. "It would," he says, "take a special kind of offer to do what I did for Shapp for someone else. I gave a year of my life for him."

Yet, Joe Napolitan proved his point—that the old-fashioned organization is no match for the new technology. Others, at the same time, were making the same point, in different ways. In Michigan, polling in 1966 became almost an exact science.

4

SCIENTIFIC POLLING:
THE ROMNEY EXPERIENCE
IN MICHIGAN

IT WAS IN APRIL OF 1962 THAT GEORGE W. ROMNEY invited
Walter D. DeVries to be his director of research. "I told him
then," says DeVries, "that I would do so only if I had what
practically amounted to carte blanche in the use of public
opinion polls. And I got it."

In mid-1967, despite two physical breakdowns, DeVries
was still working for Romney, and still ordering and inter-
preting public-opinion polls.* "We have probably made
more use of in-depth polling on issues than any political
organization in the country," DeVries argues. It is no idle
boast; it's nothing less than the simple truth. The Romney
organization in Michigan is incontestably the nation's leader
in the art of political polling.

The political technicians we have talked about up to
now have all been imaginative, alert, and willing to learn.

---

* DeVries resigned in December of 1967 for personal and professional reasons.

They have also been managers—mercenaries, in Bill Roberts's phrase. They represent one aspect of the new politics. DeVries represents another. He is a scholar who maintained a firm commitment to a political leader. DeVries earned his Ph.D. at Michigan State and actually taught political science for five years at Calvin College. While earning his doctorate, he worked as administrative assistant to the Speaker of the Michigan House of Representatives.

Why did you go into politics? I once asked DeVries. "Pure masochism," he replied. "The emerging middle ground of a profession somewhere between ward heeling and ivory tower is fascinating and, I think, significant. It improves the quality of the public debate and leads to better equipped political leaders. As a political scientist, I am interested in the development and use of factual information (empirical data, in our jargon). Both political parties need campaigns that are rational in the way they handle the candidate's time, the campaign resources, the issues, and the public-opinion polls. Perhaps the GOP has most often overlooked real public opinion. The opportunity in this party is magnificent for relating public perceptions to positive policy proposals. And let's not forget that the bulk of the American public is not basically liberal; it is moderate-conservative. With imagination and image, the GOP can capture the trust which is necessary to rise to national leadership. It is satisfying to be part of this."

DeVries, then, is no political mercenary. He is a scholar-technician who worked for more than five years for the man who best fit his own political orientation, Governor Romney. But DeVries is not an ideologue. He talks constantly of "problem-solving," a phrase that's repeated endlessly by many of the scholar-technicians who work for other moderate Republicans such as Nelson Rockefeller of New

York, Winthrop Rockefeller of Arkansas, John Love of Colorado, even Walter Hickel of Alaska. "We have twenty-five Republican governors today," says DeVries, "and all of them employ intellectuals who think for themselves. These are guys who use their brains to stay alive."

This, too, is absolutely true. Republican governors—and this is where the action is in the Republican Party, at the state houses—have been attracting bright, ambitious men like DeVries. The Democrats (with the possible exception of Pat Brown, beaten by a million votes by a movie actor) have not been attracting the same kind of people.* This trend, so subterranean that hardly anyone has commented upon it publicly, should be heartening to middle-road Republicans. (Not so heartening to right-wing Republicans, who find the whole idea of nonideological problem-solving repugnant. Without a proper ideology, they argue, you can't even isolate a problem.)

DeVries has been working to help solve George Romney's problems for a long time. In 1967 he moved out of the governor's office to work for Romney Associates, a private group established to pursue the Republican presidential nomination. Events quickly showed it would not be an easy job. Romney brought in new people and established headquarters in both Washington and Lansing. Bad feelings between the newcomers and the veterans developed almost immediately, and communication between the two headquarters was self-serving. Besides, Romney himself stumbled badly as he began to take withering fire from the national press corps. It was at this point that DeVries abruptly resigned.

---

* To be sure, Democratic intellectuals historically have worked at the national, not the state, level. Most Democratic intellectuals have been speech writers or members of issues-oriented presidential task forces. Many of them instinctively are repelled by the very idea of a scientific politics.

The apparent failure of the Romney organization to adjust to national pressures does not, however, alter the fact that it accomplished wonders in Michigan. We shall restrict our examination here to the work DeVries and others have done in-state, especially during the 1966 elections in which Romney was easily reelected along with a Republican senator and five Republican congressmen. The Michigan election was an important one, slighted as it may have been in the national press.

To set the scene:

Romney, first elected governor in 1962 and reelected in 1964, was the state's most popular political figure in 1966. By running their own state chairman, Zolton Ferency—a name no one could even pronounce—the Democrats as much as conceded defeat. The governorship, then, was not the scene for battle at all. The big race was for the Senate seat long held by Pat McNamara, a Democrat who died in office in 1966. Romney had named Robert P. Griffin, a conservative congressman (he was co-author in the House of the Landrum-Griffin bill, a dirty word to labor leaders), to fill the vacancy. Two Democrats, G. Mennen "Soapy" Williams, former six-term governor, and Jerome P. Cavanagh, mayor of Detroit, sought the Democratic nomination for that Senate seat. Williams, the best-known Democrat in Michigan, won with ease.

Thus, in the big race, it was Griffin, who was not well known to most Michigan voters, and Williams, who was known by almost everybody.

Besides that, the Democrats had won practically everything but the governorship in 1964. In particular, they had elected five bright, aggressive young men to Congress from districts that previously had been represented by Republicans. In just two years, all five of these freshmen Democrats had done wonderfully well in getting known in their home districts. Even some Republicans admitted they had been politically astute, competent, and had done their homework.

Romney, already entertaining serious ideas about running for President, found himself in a bind. Winning reelection for himself—even a whopping reelection—wasn't enough. His critics insisted he had to drag Griffin along with him plus at least some of the Republican candidates in those five congressional districts.

But hold on. Romney was a loner. He had never before worked very hard to help others running with him. And, in 1964, he had walked out on the national ticket. His refusal to support Barry Goldwater was long-established fact.

Romney insists he could not support his own national ticket in 1964 because of Goldwater's unacceptable positions on civil rights: an idealistic position no doubt in keeping with Romney's stern (and sincere) moral code. But, not entirely coincidentally, Romney's own polls proved just how practical such a stern, moral position might be.

An in-depth poll of voters' attitudes was taken in early February of 1964. A summary of the findings was written on March 26:

> No matter how you slice the stuff in Table 8 [of the computer data print-out], it's astounding. Johnson is running at a statewide approval rate of 83.9 percent. Even 76.3 percent of the Republicans approve his performance. . . .
>
> Therefore, the strategy for the Michigan campaign at this point seems clear: Democratic candidates will identify strongly with Johnson (by the time the campaign is over we'll think we ran against LBJ rather than the "gray moustache" [a reference to Neil Staebler, the Democratic candidate for governor]. They will (as in '62) play hard on the theme of party loyalty. . . . [As a result of many things], you have a serious threat to the re-election of Governor Romney. . . .

We can win if we convince (or, rather, hold) the majority of Michigan voters that Romney has been good for Michigan. The Romney administration (not the Republican Romney administration or the Romney Republican administration) has done this and will continue to build Michigan. . . . The state campaign will be overshadowed by the Presidential race—but we must do everything to keep the governor's contest from becoming embroiled in the Presidential contest both in terms of plugging the candidate and discussing national issues, except as they relate to us. . . . The Romney campaign organization must be visibly separate from the Republican operation, and it should be flexible in terms of its organization, strategy, and finances.

So advised DeVries and his research assistant, Glen Batchelder, a Michigan State doctoral candidate.

No practical man can quibble with this strategy. It was, given the circumstances, the only sure way Romney could win. And he did win, in the face of the Johnson landslide, and by a much larger margin than he had won by in 1962. If we accept the premise that the national Republican Party lost its mind in 1964 (I accept it, and so surely does Romney), the decision to cut and run was morally and practically defensible.

But it wasn't the sort of thing to encourage many people to think that Romney, in 1966, could suddenly become Michigan's Mr. Republican, the leader of a team of equally strong-willed and opinionated men.

That, however, was the decision Romney and his organization made. The governor would run as the head of an "Action Team," a *Republican* action team. He would bend all his efforts to elect Griffin and those five key Republican congressional candidates facing one-term Democrats. (There were fourteen other Republican candidates for Congress. Five of them were incumbents—one was a shoo-in for Griffin's old seat—and they really didn't need any special help. As for the other seven; well, for them, tough luck.)

Polling, or more particularly, the inspired use of polls, was a major factor in an across-the-board victory that pulled Griffin and all five congressional candidates into office. DeVries was deeply involved in the 1966 polling. But he was not the pollster. The man who polls for the Romney organization is the second key member of the team—Fred Currier, owner of Detroit's Market-Opinion Research Company.

Currier and DeVries have been working together since 1962. In that time, they have developed a rapport that helps to explain the quality of the work they perform in Romney's behalf. Both are utterly fascinated by polling; both are keenly interested in voter attitudes and the subtle refinements in those attitudes that occur in any given time span. Both, too, have been dedicated to George Romney. No comparable situation exists anywhere else.

DeVries, not at all surprisingly, is one of Currier's biggest boosters. "Currier," says DeVries, "is not only a good technician but understands the data and its relationship to campaign strategy. There aren't too many guys in the business who can do this well.

"The trouble is that often most public opinion firms are basically marketing research firms. There is a difference between testing style changes on a new Chrysler or preferences for cereal and soap, and doing a thorough in-depth study on people's political attitudes. So often political polling is such a small part of a research firm's business that it is only an avocation rather than a vocation. And there is a tendency, I think, to assign the political accounts to the more mediocre, less talented members of the firm. Also, they don't make much money on political polling.

"Currier loves political polling but he doesn't confuse

his role as technician with that of strategist. Perhaps more important, he is personally dedicated and attached to Romney, and gives an enormous amount of his time and thinking to the conduct of our campaign and administration."

Richard Helmbrecht, another member of the team, makes additional points about Currier:

"Currier is always challenging his own polls. Why, he even forces me to write critiques of the polls. He's always reading the new stuff and, besides that, he's just naturally inquisitive. His ordinary conversations sometimes sound like a regular interview. Then, too, he has developed a high sense of acceptability with the candidates. This is an especially good thing when he runs a bad [that is, unfavorable] poll."

There are, of course, all kinds of polls. It will be a long time before most political reporters forget Lyndon Johnson pulling bits and pieces of paper from his pockets and reading from them the results of the latest preferential polls from, say, Dubuque, Iowa. That, of course, was in balmier days. The preference poll is one thing. Usually, the question goes like this: "If the election were held today, who would you vote for, Johnson or Goldwater?" Or: "How do you rate the President's performance: approve or disapprove?" George Gallup and Louis Harris run these results in the newspapers all the time.

These are not the kinds of polls Currier takes and De-Vries analyzes in Michigan. Romney's polls are wide-ranging and deep-probing. "The public-opinion poll," DeVries says, "is a tool to measure what is important in a democracy— what the people think and want. It is also important in the sense that it gives the political leader, whether he is an incumbent or a candidate, a sense of direction in trying to provide leadership in solving problems. My point is that we now have technology which allows us to sample public opinion scientifically to help a political leader. Polls tell the candidate what are *relevant* issue structures, his standing with the public (the distance to the goal); and polls suggest the campaign pledges and requirements needed to develop candidate image. Polls are at least as relevant as any 'intuitive' assessment of campaign strategy—probably more so than most. And the most effective polls are in-depth image and issues polls taken over a period of time to develop a trend line and to allow campaign strategy shifts as indicated."

In other words, Romney's polls are not one-shot affairs. They all fit into a broader delineation. DeVries and Currier know what Michigan voters thought about civil rights in 1962 and in every year thereafter. They can trace the ups and downs and the changes. The Romney organization, in fact, probably has the nation's most detailed record of changing conceptions and attitudes about issues, parties, and candidates. "This is such rich stuff," says DeVries, "that we ought to write a book about it."

DeVries and Currier are interested in issues. They want to know what people are *really* thinking. But more than that: They want to know how people relate political leaders to those real issues. If the voters believe that crime is a major problem, to take an example, how do they assess George Romney's ability to deal with it? Or, to broaden it out, how do they assess the Republican Party's ability to deal with it? On those answers hangs the development of strategy. If the voters, in this hypothetical example, rate Romney's ability high and the party's ability low, keep the party out of it. If the opposite result is obtained—that is, a high rating for the party, a low rating for Romney—switch the strategy around and emphasize the party and play down the candidate.

Most organizations, once a successful campaign is concluded, collapse exhausted and bankrupt. Not the Romney organization: Two weeks after election day, these people take another in-depth poll they call an After-Election Study. The money for that poll is set aside in the regular campaign budget. So far, the temptation to dip into that cash *before* Election Day has been resisted.

Like all the other Romney polls, this one has the specific purpose of finding out what really happened. How did the campaign techniques work? What was the most effective kind of advertising? What were the most appealing issues? How did the organization function?

The first major study looking forward to the 1966 election was taken in November and December of 1965. That poll attempted to measure Romney's appeal to the voters, the issues the voters considered important as they were related to the candidates and to the party, and the voters' reaction to the Republican Party in Michigan compared to the national Republican Party. Additionally, the poll, through secret ballots, pitted the leading Republican candidates for the Senate against the Democratic incumbent, Pat McNamara, who at the time the poll was taken was still alive. Romney was also given a test run against the two leading Democrats in the state, "Soapy" Williams and Jerome Cavanagh.

This poll is worth examining in some detail because it is reasonably typical of the Romney organization's work and is a good introduction to some of the organization's specialized techniques.

"Hello," the mimeographed form begins, "I'm Mrs. ——— from Market-Opinion Research Company, and we are making a study of problems facing Michigan." Note that no mention of the client is made. The reason, of course, is that if the person being interviewed knew the poll was being taken for Romney, the responses might be biased.

First question: "Are you a registered voter in Michigan? followed by a box for "yes" and a box for "no." If the answer is "no," the interviewer is told to discontinue the interview. The reasons for that are obvious enough.

Next question: "What are the *most important* problems facing Michigan at the present time?" Six blank lines are included for the interviewer to write down the answers.

"What do you feel is the most important *single* problem facing Michigan?"

"What do you think ought to be done about this problem?"

Note here that all these questions are open-end, meaning that the person being interviewed can pick his own answers in his own words. Note, too, that the questions are all framed in such a way that they don't hint at the bias, if there is any, of the survey itself. Furthermore, these open-end questions are designed to relax the respondent and get him talking.

The wording of questions in a poll is of absolutely vital importance. "The questionnaire," says Fred Currier, "is a straight function of length, and the real clue is to use questions that are clear, simple, elegant, and cannot be in any way misunderstood. This is far from easy; it is, of course, an art. Stanley L. Payne's *The Art of Asking Questions,* a minor classic, points out how differences in words and wording will change data; the range is between 10 and 40 percent. So all questions, particularly if you're starting out with an open-end question, should be very simple, and allow the person being interviewed to go in any direction he wants.

"A typical open-end question might be, 'What do you believe are the most important problems facing our nation this year?' Then, after you've asked that one, you can go on to another simple open-end question, such as 'Well, what do you think should be done about this?' You can, in your techniques, go on from that, a completely open-ended, unstructured question, to a semistructured question where you may have a two-way choice, and on up to a three- or four-way semistructured question. Then, finally, you can begin scaling the questions.

"All question techniques, in terms of attitude research, are basically two-dimensional—that is, you can ask only about how one person perceives a thing or an institution on a dimension that runs from verbal anchors of very positive polar attributes.

"It's easy to ask a bad question. Taking the example I've already used, you'd have a bad question if you asked, 'What do you believe *should be* the most important problems facing our nation this year?' There is always bias in any question; I think that's obvious. The most simple questions in the world are one word or just a few words, such as 'Oh?' or 'Is that so?' or, taking an example from Payne's book, 'Sex?' Even those questions, obviously enough, can be misinterpreted."

The Romney organization takes no chances in its polling. Every poll is pretested. Says Currier: "The best way is not to have one of your best interviewers pretest, but to go out and do it yourself—and in a real sticky, tough area."

But back to the poll itself. Next question: "How do you think things are going in our state capital at Lansing?" Boxes reading "excellent," "good," "fair," "poor," and "don't know" are included. The question, then, is semistructured. The next question is open-end: "What do you mean by that?" Again, space is provided to write down the answer.

So far, simple questions, traditional techniques. Now, however, the fun begins. The interviewer is instructed to show the interviewee "Card A" listing some of the problems presumably facing Michigan. The interviewer is then instructed to say: "This card also [besides listing the questions] has a scale from '0' for *not at all important* to '10' for *very important,* with the in-between values also represented by numbers. How would you rate each of these issues?" The issues listed were: taxes, job situation—creating jobs, state finances, civil rights, education, tax reform, crime and delinquency, mental health, medical care for older people, and concern for all types of voters.

Next, the poll attempts to relate Romney to these issues. The question: "How would you rate Romney on his ability to solve these issues and problems?" The interviewer is instructed to show the interviewee "Card B" and then explain: "This card has a scale very similar to the one you have just used except '0' means *not at all able* and '10' means *very able.* The same problems are listed, each prefixed by the word "handling" (as in "handling tax reform").

Next question: "Do you approve or disapprove of the way Governor Romney is handling his job?" with boxes supplied for the answers. Then the abrupt question "Why?" with room supplied for the open-end answer. Finally, to measure the intensity of the response, this question: "How strongly do you feel about your answer?"

The poll then moves on to ask pretty much the same kinds of questions about national issues, using again the same "Card A" and "Card B" techniques. The emphasis on Vietnam, however, is interesting, in light of Romney's personal problems in handling that tricky question.

One type of question not included in this particular poll, but now a part of all Romney polls, is the semantic differential. In this technique, the person being interviewed is given a sheet of paper. Taking as an example an actual semantic differential used in a later Romney poll, the person being interviewed would see something like this:

GEORGE ROMNEY

interesting	___; ___; ___ □ ___; ___; ___	uninteresting
experienced	___; ___; ___ □ ___; ___; ___	inexperienced
quarrelsome	___; ___; ___ □ ___; ___; ___	congenial
trained	___; ___; ___ □ ___; ___; ___	untrained
bold	___; ___; ___ □ ___; ___; ___	timid
dishonest	___; ___; ___ □ ___; ___; ___	honest
passive	___; ___; ___ □ ___; ___; ___	active
safe	___; ___; ___ □ ___; ___; ___	dangerous
uninformed	___; ___; ___ □ ___; ___; ___	informed
meek	___; ___; ___ □ ___; ___; ___	aggressive
just	___; ___; ___ □ ___; ___; ___	unjust
unqualified	___; ___; ___ □ ___; ___; ___	qualified
frank	___; ___; ___ □ ___; ___; ___	reserved
liberal	___; ___; ___ □ ___; ___; ___	conservative

The idea of a semantic differential is to measure the profile—the respondent's perceptions—of an organization or a candidate. "The semantic differential," says Fred Currier, "is merely a polar opposite set of words, from good to bad. One of the reasons that it's better than multiple-choice questions is that it gives you many more dimensions that can be factor-analyzed and that can be related across party-attitude data and candidate-attitude data. It's one of the most sensitive scales, and it has polar opposites in the words by which many candidates and parties are measured—*good-bad, honest-dishonest, safe-dangerous, liberal-conservative, frank-reserved.* Words like these do come up when people are describing parties and candidates.

"The semantic differential has had more academic, technical work done on it, probably, than any other attitudinal measurement tool in recent years. It's one of the most useful devices we've found to measure candidate images and party images over a period of time, and we've built it in at this level for the past six years [1962 through 1967], so that we have a storehouse of data on this technique in terms of both parties in Michigan and most major candidates."

The final questions in every Romney poll are especially noteworthy. Here, the person being interviewed is asked (as he was in our example) how he voted in the presidential elections in 1964 and 1960, in the county race for sheriff in 1964 and 1962, and in the elections for secretary of state and attorney general in 1964.

This is not just idle curiosity. What the poll is trying to do is separate the straight party voters from what the Romney people call the "ticket splitters." The ticket-splitter concept is fundamental to the whole Romney campaign approach. And it is still controversial.

The traditional polling technique is to allow the person being interviewed to define his own voting instincts. Thus, this sort of question: "What do you consider yourself, a Republican, a Democrat, or an Independent?" Or: "Do you lean to the Republican or Democratic Party?"

This self-administered definition, DeVries argues, "is not related to behavior or to a time dimension."

In a letter to Robert Taft, Jr., dated October 12, 1964 (just days before the Johnson-Goldwater election), DeVries and Batchelder made these interesting points:

1. If our polls (and those of Gallup, Roper, *et al*) are accurate, ticket-splitting in this election will be the highest ever. [It was: Johnson carried Michigan by 1,000,000 votes; Romney was elected governor by 400,000 votes.]
2. What is true in Michigan is also reflected in the coun-

try. In Michigan, for example, about 35 percent of our voters split their tickets in 1962. Now, this compares to a straight 1962 Democratic vote of about 40 percent and a straight Republican vote of 25 percent (nationally, the Democratic vote is about 40 percent, GOP about 23 percent, and ticket-splitters about 37 percent).

3. In Michigan's 1962 election, 40 percent of the voters were normally straight Democratic, yet Governor Romney took 8.5 percent of that vote. Romney also took 68 percent of the ticket-splitters' votes (who account for 35 percent of THE TOTAL) and 96 percent of the 25 percent of the electorate who normally vote straight Republican. Thus, over half of the Romney vote came from other than straight Republican voters.

4. In five of the last six Presidential elections, Michigan voters gave victory margins to Presidential candidates of one party and gubernatorial candidates of the other party.

5. We define a ticket-splitter as one who deviates from his traditional party behavior at the Presidential or gubernatorial level. In Michigan it would be anyone who voted a straight party ticket for the Administrative Board candidates (e.g., secretary of state, attorney general, etc.) and local candidates, but who split off in the vote for governor and/or President. We use the attorney general as the index of straight party voting.

Ticket-splitting, at the precinct level, is computed by comparing the attorney general candidate's percentage of the vote in that race with the gubernatorial candidate's percentage in his race. For example, if the Republican candidate for attorney general received 40 percent of a precinct's vote and the gubernatorial candidate garnered 48 percent, this represents a rather high deviation of 8 percent. In Michigan, the differences run from 0 percent in many rural precincts and some small cities to a high of 10 percent in the suburban areas of the Detroit metropolitan area. Generally, we find that the closer you move to our three-county metropolitian area, the higher the incidence of ticket-splitting. In Detroit itself, ticket-splitting is highest on the outskirts of the city and decreases as you move toward the city's core. While high ticket-splitting is characteristic of the Detroit metropolitan area, the same is not always true of other large cities out-state.

We have also discovered the following things about the characteristics of those who split their tickets. First, there are more people in this category all the time. Second, the majority of them generally side with the winner and actually give him his margin of victory. The voter who says he is undecided in pre-election polls is, more often than not, a ticket-splitter when he does vote. We find there are two distinct groups of ticket-splitters:

A. The opinion leader. This voter is sensitive to news media and takes time to inform himself of the issues. He is generally not involved in party activity, although he may perform some election-day function (clerk, poll watcher, etc.). This ticket-splitter is basically suburban, middle class, and white collar.

B. The waverer. This ticket-splitter is less issue-oriented. He is basically indifferent to the political arena and the media coverage of it. He is apt to be lower middle class and he makes up his mind at the last minute about casting his ballot.

Our basic conclusion is that elections are won or lost by the voting behavior of those who are neither doctrinaire Republicans or Democrats, but who split their tickets. In reaching this voting group, it is important to consider very carefully both the candidate and the issues. Our experience in Michigan also tells us that middle-road candidates, deeply committed to no particular interest bloc, have considerable appeal to this ticket-splitter.

This ticket-splitter can be located through election-return analyses. The strategy is then to concentrate money, effort, and candidate presence in those areas of heavy ticket-splitting. Instruction in how to split your vote can be included in the literature aimed at these pockets of ticket-splitting. It is also helpful to have organizations, such as our Romney Volunteers, which co-ordinate the support of those not closely identified with the party machinery. These are given special emphasis in ticket-splitter territory. Campaign material for these areas stresses the candidate and the issues more than party affiliation. This is sometimes called scientific politics, but it would seem more pertinent to call it recognition of political reality. The goal is to attract the ever-increasing number of voters who are not doctrinaire party followers.

Polls, such as the one we have been analyzing, are not used to find where ticket-splitters congregate. That, as De-Vries notes, is done by election-return analyses, an immensely complicated and time-consuming job that is eased in Michigan by the use of computers.

The polls, however, do show what kind of people the ticket-splitters are and what they are thinking. The polls also help to determine precisely how they plan to vote.

No poll is any better than the sample—the cross section —that's interviewed. Choosing the sample is just as important as framing the questions. In the poll we've been examining, the sample was 820 people, divided equally between men and women. Everyone interviewed was a registered voter (or, at least, claimed to be).

Interviews were taken in 14 "heavyweight" counties and 5 rural counties. A "heavyweight" county is simply a populous, high-vote county that has tended over the years to favor Romney. There are 83 counties in Michigan, and 19 of them are categorized as "heavyweight." In 1964, Romney received 81 percent of his vote from these counties; the comparable figure in 1962 was 78 percent. The Romney sample, as a result, is primarily taken from these heavyweight counties. Each campaign, too, is concentrated in these areas.

By trial and error, the Romney people have determined that this kind of heavyweight-oriented sample is most appropriate to their needs. In the poll we have been examining, the heaviest interviewing schedule was in Wayne County (which includes Detroit), where seven interviews were completed in each of 40 blocks selected on a "probability" basis. Probability means the selection has been completely random. It is scientific in the sense that the choice is wide enough and the interviewing schedule heavy enough to presuppose a representative cross section. A probability sample is one of two basic types; the second is the quota-control sample in which specific types of people are chosen for interviewing to *guarantee* a representative cross section. A quota-control sample, in other words, would be a microcosm of the community at large. If the county was 25 percent Catholic, for example, one out of four persons interviewed would be Catholic. The trouble with that kind of sample is that the interviewer often finds the person he or she is assigned to interview is not at home. The interviewer, as a result, may have to make three or four callbacks. Ordinarily, the additional costs involved in quota-sampling make the technique prohibitive, to political pollsters anyway. Normally, a Romney statewide poll consists of some 1,000 to 1,250 interviews (a bit higher than the one we have considered). The standard error is in the range of 2 to 3 percent, which is acceptable to the Romney organization in all but the closest contests.*

What were the results of the poll we have been considering? First, that Romney was widely admired by the voters. A remarkable 78.6 percent approved the way he was handling his job, including 66 percent of the Democrats, 84.8 percent of the ticket-splitters, and 90.6 percent of the Republicans. The Romney people might have guessed that, of course: But, thanks to the poll, they were now certain. Second, that a new issue had grabbed the voters' attention—crime and delinquency. In a similar poll in 1964, that issue

---

* There's an interesting rule of thumb about cutting this standard margin of error: To cut it in half, you must increase the size of the sample four times; that is, by the square of the error. Most pollsters figure it's not worth the additional costs to do so.

ranked seventh, mentioned in response to an open-end question by only 1 percent of the voters. In 1965 it was first, voluntarily mentioned by 25.2 percent of the voters. Finances/fiscal reform, which had ranked first in 1964, had dropped in 1965 to sixth. Romney's analysts agreed that voters were satisfied the governor had faced up to this problem and helped to solve it.

The overall figures were significant. But, for the Romney experts, the breakdowns by voting category—Republican, Democratic, and ticket-splitter—may have been even more significant. Unemployment, for example, was mentioned as a problem by only 7.4 percent of the Republicans. The figure for Democrats, however, was 11.1 percent, and, for ticket-splitters, 10.6 percent. On finances/fiscal reform, Republicans were aroused. But Democrats barely mentioned it.

The answers to the question "What do you think should be done about this problem?" are revealing too. On crime and delinquency, 31.9 percent suggested stricter law enforcement. But the figure for the Republicans was 40.9 percent; for Democrats, 27 percent; for ticket-splitters, 32.7 percent. More police protection and more policemen were the second most popular remedy, mentioned by a total of 24.2 percent. But the figure for Republicans was only 6.8 percent. For Democrats, the figure climbed sharply to 36 percent. For ticket-splitters, it was 23.6 percent.

The poll also emphasized Griffin's problems as a candidate for the Senate. In answer to the question "Who do you think would be the strongest Republican candidate for senator?" he finished fourth, behind Romney, Congressman Gerald Ford, and John Hannah, president of Michigan State University. More significantly, of 820 persons interviewed, he was mentioned by only 17.

Another question, "What would you say are Robert P.

Griffin's strengths?" could hardly have given Griffin much comfort. There were 401 persons who said they'd never heard of him and 313 who said they didn't know any of his strengths.

We have mentioned two problems that occur in every poll—framing the questions and choosing the sample. There is now a third that is just as serious—coding the replies. It is especially difficult in a poll that uses a quantity of open-end questions. The coder must reduce the words of the respondent into neatly compartmentalized subdivisions that can be punched on a card that will then be fed into a computer.

"You start with a sample of your whole survey," says Fred Currier, "and see what the coders are coming up with in terms of thought groups in answer to the questions. Now, when you ask an open-end question, what you're trying to find is a dynamic. What is the real causal operation going on in a person's mind when they come to a decision as to, say, What is the main problem facing the nation? Why is it the main problem? What would you do about the problem if you could do something about it? So you find they say, 'Riots in the streets are caused by too much progress in the civil-rights movement.' 'What would you do about it?' 'Enforce police power.' 'Why would you enforce police power?' 'Because the police have their hands tied.' Things like this. You want to hold the thought groups together so they make sense. A good example of this is the civil-rights data which has broken down in the last few years into three or four areas, all sort of keyed together. And, as an issue structure like this begins to break down and become larger in total, your code data has to be broken down. Now, the trick on this is to be sure that you somehow have comparable classes of coding groups. You want to have the same thought ideas coded for comparison when you make future studies. Of course, this isn't always possible because the belief structure may not always be comparable, but that is the aim.

"There's room for error in this process. The coding crew is set on the sample codes; then they go through and code the whole study. At that time, the study is sent to key punching and it's punched up. There is room for error from the source document to the coding; there's room for error from coding to punching. Each of these has to be controlled, and they can be controlled to a large extent. When we get to the punching level, we normally make two or three quick runs [on the computer] to take a look at the data before we run it through the computer completely. That way, we don't come up with too many surprises."

There is, then, this progression. The interviewers turn in their completed forms. The coder takes those forms and reduces the answers to each question to symbols. Each interview, now reduced to symbols, is turned over to a key puncher. He punches them out on a card. The cards are fed into the computer. The computer prints out the results.

It is at this point that Currier sits down with DeVries and his group to go over all of the so-called straight-run data. "At that time," says Currier, "we usually write up some sort of an analysis and then come back and list eight or ten or twelve cross-runs and any other further analysis we might want to do."

One example of a cross-run might be the statistical relationship between what undecided voters think about the crime problem as compared to committed Romney voters. Another might be a breakdown of ticket-splitters' perceptions of Romney's ability to handle the civil-rights problem. Given a high-speed computer's immense capabilities, almost anything is possible.

The first meeting between Currier and the DeVries

team usually lasts two or three hours. "We sit around all afternoon reading the questionnaires and just soaking up the data. You let the data talk to you; you never try to talk to it. Just sit there and let the stuff wash over you up to your neck and try to wash your mind clean of preconceptions, saying to yourself, 'Now what are these people really trying to tell us about this situation.' "

DeVries is equally high on this approach. He is especially sold on the idea of reading the actual filled-in questionnaires, or at least a sampling of them. By reading the actual words of the people interviewed, Currier and DeVries feel, they are able to get a much better idea of what's behind the symbols taken from the raw data. Further, by reading the actual interviews, they can get a measurement of intensity.

Currier and DeVries have worked together so long that they hardly need to explain anything to each other. Currier doesn't have to "sell" what's in his polls, and DeVries doesn't have to be taught what the data means. The two men, and their associated experts, almost always agree on the significance of the polls, and they have little trouble writing an analysis that they can pass along to Romney. The governor himself, largely because of limitations upon his time, rarely sits in on the meetings that consider the raw data. "Of course," says DeVries, "a candidate must give his attention to poll results or there is no point in going through the motions. He absolutely must see the poll analyses (not the raw data) and base overall strategy on the kinds of facts discovered. Some candidates become intrigued by the computer print-outs and begin spouting jargon. Romney doesn't do this; he is adept at reading data and spotting significant trends. You must remember that George Romney had a good deal of familiarity with market research as head of

American Motors. But his time is limited, and so we highlight the data for him."

Other candidates, including some of the men who ran in those five key congressional races in Michigan in 1966, aren't sophisticated about polls. Dealing with such men presents a whole new set of problems.

"A candidate like this," says Currier, "brings up questions about whether he can accept the data because of the sample size and whether it all fits into his preconceptions. If he's in the middle of a campaign, he wonders whether he can do anything about what you're able to tell him.

"In many cases, this kind of meeting may take all afternoon, and the candidate will walk around the room, smoking a cigar, basically upset by the situation, especially if it shows him lower than he thought he was. This kind of soul-searching with a candidate, I think, is an extremely difficult problem because it involves a unique situation in market research—that is, explaining to the person who's being measured that these are accurate measurements of himself. It's often very difficult psychologically for him to accept. Think, for example, of the problem of a candidate who has been in public life, in the legislature or the state senate, say, for twenty years, and you tell him hardly anyone has ever heard of him. So, if there's any way out of it, I normally try to work with a staff person and not the candidate. It's not wise, I think, to communicate directly with the candidate at all times."

Currier has delivered more than a few unfavorable polls to candidates.* Unsophisticated candidates, he has found,

---

* Currier pulls no punches in his polling analysis. This is because he is accepted in Michigan, and highly respected. Other pollsters, some of them well known nationally, tend to sugar-coat their findings to please their clients. They reason that if they keep turning in acceptable polls they'll be hired the next time. They should, of course, be fired.

react in two ways: They take the polls too lightly or they take them too seriously.

In 1966 some of the candidates saw that their position was not good "in terms of overall strength, and so they refused to accept the data. They neglected to act on definite recommendations about what areas they needed to campaign in, what issues were important in these areas, and what they needed to say to specific groups. In one case, a congressional candidate failed to act on this data. A second poll was taken for him and for the other four congressional candidates. It showed that the other four had moved up about 10 points each by acting on the recommendations. But he hadn't moved at all. This is a case where a candidate took the polls too lightly and didn't gear up his organization to move. He ultimately did win the district, but only after a lot of last-minute work.

"In cases where candidates have taken the polls too seriously—that is, in cases where the candidate was behind when he expected to be ahead—I've seen two reactions. In one, he'll sit facing the wall and start drinking whisky, and things really start to fall apart. So I've found you have to temper your words and watch the candidate very carefully when you're giving him this material. In other cases, the candidate and his whole group get together and rededicate themselves. They begin to grind, almost too heavily, on the basis of the data they have seen. Too heavily in the sense that maybe the poll is *not* that accurate. But at least it gets them off and going at a much more frantic level."

When polls are favorable, one after another, everything drops into place. This was what happened in Griffin's Senate race; he kept showing gains in each succeeding poll. "This dramatic rise of Griffin in periodic polls," says DeVries, "allowed the massive infusion of life into his campaign that made the difference. Favorable polls are magical fund-raising and organizational tools!"

So let us now, for a moment, recapitulate.

We have seen how a good poll is made, how it's taken, and how it's analyzed. In a general way, we've examined what the Romney polls prior to the 1966 election showed. Chiefly, the results were these: Romney continued to maintain his remarkable popularity; the rest of the candidates weren't nearly so well known; voter interest in issues was changing, basically from an interest in economic matters to social problems.

The question now became how to capitalize upon the data turned up by the polls. This problem broke down in two ways—organizing a campaign for Griffin, where national issues were mostly relevant, and organizing the campaigns for five congressional candidates, where local issues were often preponderant.

Thanks to the use of semantic differentials, the strategy for Griffin's campaign became obvious as soon as the Democrats selected "Soapy" Williams as their candidate. "We took a liberal-conservative scale," says Currier. For Democratic voters, it looked like this:

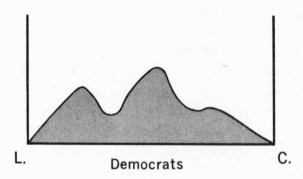

L.   Democrats   C.

For Republican voters, this is how it looked:

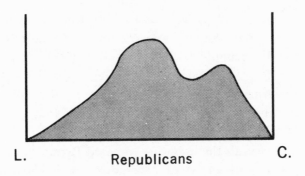

L.   **Republicans**   C.

Most voters associated with both parties, in other words, placed themselves in the middle. That accomplished, Currier asked these same voters to place Griffin and Williams on the same scale. Griffin was placed smack in the middle—where the votes are—by both Republicans and Democrats. Williams, however, was positioned far to the left, where there were some Democrats but hardly any Republicans.

There was, however, this additional situation: Voters were sure of their decision when they put Williams far to the left. Most were only guessing when they put Griffin in the middle. They knew—or thought they knew—about Williams; they didn't know much about Griffin. "Attitudes about Griffin," says Currier, "were a blank page. It was our job to fill up that page with information."

The "information" had to be that Griffin was in fact a moderate, even though most impartial observers who knew his background would have agreed he was rather conservative. This is just what happened. Romney's staff pushed hard to force Griffin to take moderate positions. Griffin's own staff, as a matter of fact, pushed him in that direction. Ultimately, people who participated in the campaign say that he agreed to move to the center, even though his original inclination was to hold fast to his conservative beliefs.

One issue was paramount—Griffin's co-authorship of the Landrum-Griffin bill, which most labor leaders categorize as reactionary. The Republicans hit the issue head on in brochures and pamphlets. It was a good bill for everybody, including labor, they said. Brochures even showed a photograph of Griffin "consulting" with John F. Kennedy. Kennedy, the cutline said, "praised Bob for his great contribution to labor."

Otherwise, all the literature pictured Romney and Griffin as partners in a progressive-action team. Griffin stressed those issues turned up in the polls. He was pictured as being for better education, improved rapid transit, low-cost housing, controls to eliminate air and water pollution. Above all, campaign literature played him up as a problem-solver.

All this posed a two-headed problem for Williams. First, he had to demonstrate he was not a *far*-left liberal, which in truth he was not. Second, he had to document that Griffin was a leaner to the Goldwater right, which in fact Griffin was. Williams never proved either point, and lost. His indecision was most graphically demonstrated by his statement that he wasn't sure how he would have voted on the Landrum-Griffin bill had he been in the Congress at the time.

It was again an election in which one side (the Republicans) relied heavily on a mass-media campaign, and the other (the Democrats) continued to rely chiefly on old-fashioned organization, although, it should be said, the contrast wasn't as stark as in the Pennsylvania primary.

The five congressional races were another matter altogether. The Democratic incumbents had no obvious incumbrances, except that they were running in a year that turned out to favor Republicans generally. All of them were good, solid performers who had won the respect and even

admiration of those who had come to know them or something about them. The Republicans were generally unknown and untested. All things being even, most of the
Democrats should have won.

Once again, however, the Republicans showed what
inspired mass-media techniques—all of them hooked into
polling—can accomplish. Then, too, the Republicans went
hunting where the ducks were.

For each of the five districts, the Romney organization
prepared computer print-outs giving the results of the 1964
election by precinct and noting in each precinct the level of
ticket-splitting. "Campaign resources," said the foreword to
each of the sets of print-outs, "should be allocated to each
place in the district in a methodical way. The most essential
of these is the time of the candidate; it should therefore be
used carefully. So should other limited resources, such as
money, advertising, and mailings."

Congressional candidates were urged to parcel out their
time just as methodically as Romney and Griffin were parcel-
ing out theirs. The Romney organization has worked out a
scientific method for alloting campaign time. Each campaign
day is divided into three parts: mornings, afternoons, and
evenings. Each county is then studied to determine what
proportion of the total vote it contributed in the most relevant preceding election and what proportion of that vote it
gave Romney.

A typical time-assignment sheet starts out this way:

GENESSEE COUNTY
Contribution ratio:
    State: 4.49 percent
    Romney: 4.20 percent

Total vote: 124,254
Romney: 59,674

The importance of Genessee County is then placed in scientific perspective. It is assigned so many units of time directly in proportion to the contribution it may be expected to make. Romney, on the basis of this data, spent three mornings, two afternoons, and two evenings in Genessee County. As early as August 12, many of those appearances were assigned. Thus:

First Morning

FLINT: 52.61 percent [of the county's] population; 46.1 percent Romney; 3.8 percent ticket-splitters.
1. Factory gate.
2. Breakfast—Romney volunteers and Republican leaders.
3. Press conference.
4. Plant tours.
5. Restaurants—coffee shops.
6. Community college.

MT. MORRIS Township: 5.51 percent population; 41.6 percent Romney; 5.5 percent ticket-splitters.
1. Door-to-door in precincts 2, 4, 5.
2. Lunch—restaurant drop-in.

BURTON Township: 7.93 percent population; 41.4 percent Romney; 4.1 percent ticket-splitters.
1. Door-to-door in precincts 4, 6, 7, 12, 13, 14, 19, 20.
2. Neighborhood rally in any of the above precincts.

The precincts assigned for door-to-door visits were not chosen at random; they were chosen because they had the highest incidence of ticket-splitting in earlier elections. The Romney organization knew this, and it also knew from polls just what issues were paramount in the voters' minds.*

---

* This sort of thing can be carried to extremes. In Colorado, Governor John Love, in his door-to-door visits, knew from canvassing what issues were relevant in *each household*.

Scientific scheduling also applied to Griffin's campaign. The scheduling of Mrs. Romney and Mrs. Griffin was almost as scientific.

No congressional candidate can ordinarily allot his time quite so scientifically as this. First of all, he isn't running for governor or senator; he just isn't so important that he can dictate when and where he will appear or precisely how long he will stay. But this was the kind of example that was set for these five candidates in Michigan, and most of them did their best to live up to it.

When they did appear, these candidates almost invariably addressed themselves to *relevant* issues. Once again, that was made possible by the polls. At least two polls were taken in each of the congressional districts, and they were illuminating.

The candidate in the Second Congressional District was Marvin Esch; his Democratic opponent was Wes Vivian. The first poll showed 46.9 percent of the voters supporting Vivian, 29.5 percent for Esch, and the rest undecided.

That same poll showed some interesting patterns in voters' attitudes toward issues. In Monroe City, for example, 29 percent of the voters listed water pollution as an issue. In Ann Arbor, only 4.9 percent mentioned pollution. But, in Ann Arbor, home of the University of Michigan, schools/ teachers/education was mentioned by 39.2 percent of the voters. Back in Monroe City, only 18 percent talked about education.

Esch did precisely what the data suggested. He prepared a special brochure detailing his positive position on water pollution, and saw that it was distributed to *every* household in Monroe City. In Ann Arbor, he talked and talked about education.

In Lenawee County, education was mentioned as a

major issue by 74 percent of the voters, and for a good reason: Teachers were working day to day without contracts, and were threatening to go on strike. The situation was explosive, with highly concerned voters taking strong positions. Esch took no position favoring either side. He simply noted that he had been a member of the education and labor committee in the state House of Representatives and that labor relations was his specialty. "Let's reason together," he said.

In another county, a plan was under consideration to consolidate dozens of school districts into four regional districts. Farmers were especially outraged by the plan. Heeding the advice of the polling analysts, Esch got as far away from that one as he could.

The Romney organization came up with all kinds of specialized techniques to help the congressmen. The five campaigns became, in fact, almost a campaign laboratory experiment. Each technique was carefully market-tested.

The most effective technique probably was the recorded phone call. It was used in different ways in different districts, in an effort to determine the best format. In Esch's district, letters under Romney's signature were sent to selected households in ticket-splitting precincts. The letters said that Romney would be telephoning them in a few days.

Three machines were used in Esch's district. They work this way: An operator dials the number, waits until a light goes on to signal that someone has answered, and then switches on the recorded message. While the message is running, he moves on to dial another number. One machine, this way, can make 2,500 calls a day.

"Hello," the transcribed message begins, "this is Governor Romney." The governor then proceeds to discuss the campaign, and conclude with a plug for the local candidate for Congress.

Variations were tried and tested. In one of these, the governor gave his pitch and then introduced the congressional candidate, who followed up with a short pitch of his own. In another variation, the candidate did all the talking. In still another, the candidate concluded by asking the person listening to him to call a special number at headquarters and voice his complaints. That technique was tried in Esch's district until the candidate found he was spending almost all his time at the end of a telephone receiver. Thereafter, the calls were taken by a member of the staff.

The original two machines used in Esch's district completed 52,213 calls. Under a contract with Telectraphonics Corp., owner of the equipment, the charge was four cents a call. When polling and market-testing showed the technique was having a significant impact, a third machine was rushed to the district for the last eight days of the campaign. That machine completed 9,308 calls; the charge was five cents a call, payable again to Telectraphonics.

Five other machines were used, two in Gary Brown's Third District and three in Jack McDonald's Nineteenth. They completed a total of 84,237 calls. All together, then, the machines completed calls to 145,758 households (most of them located in heavy ticket-splitting neighborhoods) in three key congressional districts. Romney strategists believe the calls probably supplied the margin of victory in two of the three districts—Esch's and McDonald's.

The Romney organization also made significant efforts to capture nominally Democratic votes in Negro precincts, especially in Detroit. Borrowing from Lindsay's New York City campaign (see Chapter Seven), the Romney organization, through its Operation Grass Roots, established a number of neighborhood headquarters. But instead of renting space in empty storefronts, the Romney people managed to recruit individuals who opened their own houses as headquarters. A special banner was prepared; it shows Romney side by side with . . . Abraham Lincoln. Small rallies were held regularly at these headquarters; larger pep rallies were held at schools and playgrounds, where Romney T-shirts and Griffin headbands were distributed to the kids.

"The results were indicative of what can be done in the Negro community," a summary report noted. "There is still a tremendous amount of enthusiasm in this area, which should certainly be developed by the Republican Party." It hardly needs to be added that some of these Negro precincts were ravaged in the tragic rioting of July, 1967.

Another volunteer program was called Women-Out-Working; the acronym is WOW. Upside down, it spells MOM. No more need be said.

There was much, much more. Television, for example, was used heavily, and most of it was market-tested before the campaign began. The impact of Romney's walking tours was studied.* An area in Detroit called Test City was studied to determine how the campaign's urban-directed issues were being accepted. Other "weathervane" precincts around the state were analyzed. Statistics on the probability of voter turnout were compiled.

The campaign's effectiveness is measured by the final results. They were:

Romney, 1,490,430; Ferency, 963,383.
Griffin, 1,363,630; Williams, 1,069,484.

---

* The number of hands he shook was actually counted on one such tour. The total was 265. The next day, pollsters asked residents of the neighborhood if they had met Romney and if they had shaken his hand. 800 said they had.

And in those five key congressional races:

Second District: Esch, 65,205; Vivian, 62,536.
Third District: Brown, 68,912; Todd, 62,984.
Seventh District: Riegle, 71,166; Mackie, 60,408.
Eleventh District: Ruppe, 70,820; Clevenger, 65,875.
Nineteenth District: McDonald, 76,884; Farnum, 57,907.

It was a clean sweep. There were a number of ironies about it. First, it was largely neglected by the national press. To that, I plead guilty. Shortly after the 1966 elections, I wrote an analysis of Nelson Rockefeller's campaign; I described it as almost perfect. DeVries doesn't agree; he believes that the 1966 Michigan campaign is to date the best example of the new politics in action. He may be right, although I still tend to believe that the Rockefeller campaign was more creative and more imaginative. Second, there is the irony of this brilliantly academic-scientific campaign being run in behalf of George Romney, the least formally educated leader in the Republican Party.

It seems clear at this writing that Romney has not fully grasped the significance of these new techniques. His efforts to move out of Michigan and onto a national stage have been lackluster. In expanding his staff, he hired new people who immediately came into conflict with those veterans who had served him so well. "Egos," said one of these veterans, "lie bleeding here on the floor." And DeVries resigned.

Romney, it seemed safe to say, would not be that candidate who would put together the first thoroughly modern presidential campaign.

But the 1966 election in Michigan will stand for years to come as one of the first thoroughly modern statewide political campaigns. And, on that point, this needs to be said:

It was an organizational effort, but it was not put together by a regular party organization. That 1966 campaign was the work of George Romney's personal political organization, an organization that had grown so large and become so effective that, by 1966, it had replaced the old, hidebound party structure that ran Michigan Republican affairs—badly —for so many years.

It was another personal organization that ran a brilliant and thoroughly modern political campaign in New York in 1966, and we shall now examine Nelson Rockefeller's uses of political power.

5

INSPIRED TELEVISION:
NELSON ROCKEFELLER
IN NEW YORK

On January 3, 1967, Nelson A. Rockefeller repeated, for the third time in nine years, those familiar words: "I do solemnly swear that I will . . . faithfully discharge the duties of the office of governor to the best of my ability."

Sweet words for a much-traveled man hardly anyone thought could be elected to a third four-year term as governor of New York. And costly words. To win that reelection, some $260,000 was spent to make each of those twenty-two little words possible.

Nelson Rockefeller's winning campaign in 1966 was probably the most expensive nonpresidential campaign ever put together in America. Not only the most expensive, but one of the most professional, one of the most astute, one of the most imaginative. And one of the most ruthless.

The sheer size of the Rockefeller campaign was staggering:

1. By my own count, 3,027 Rockefeller commercials

were shown on New York's 22 commercial television stations. The actual total, because of reporting inconsistencies,
may have run as high as 4,000.

2. By the Rockefeller organization's count, some 27,-
000,000 brochures, buttons, and broadsides were distributed
to the voters. That's about 4½ items for every person who
turned out to vote.

3. Rockefeller himself, traveling by bus, by jet airplane, by helicopter, and even by seaplane, visited all 62
counties in the state. In August alone, he shook thousands
of hands at 17 county fairs in upstate New York. Wherever
he went, he was able to keep in constant radio touch with
his 84-room headquarters spread over two floors at New York
City's Hilton Hotel.

"Never again," says one of Rockefeller's strategists,
"will we see another campaign like it." That's probably not
true; someone else one day will spend as much money and
spend it just as well. And, almost certainly, the techniques
Rockefeller used in New York will be built into the nation's first new-style presidential campaign.

What the Rockefeller strategist means is that never
again will anyone see another Rockefeller campaign like it.
Maybe not; Nelson Rockefeller says 1966 was his last hurrah. Thwarted twice in seeking the Presidency, he had
decided in 1967 to put his national ambitions aside and
work, however unwillingly, for George Romney.

On the face of it, that seemed absurd.* Nelson Rockefeller, in late 1967, was the picture of rugged good health.
He had finally become a professional campaigner, and his

---

* Others were beginning to think so too. As this is written, a
ground swell of modest dimensions is beginning to form for Rockefeller. Most observers, however, doubted it could sweep Rockefeller
into the White House.

staff had mastered the new scientific politics. The Rockefeller organization was at the top of its political form.

Whatever happens to Rockefeller, this much is certain: He leaves a rich political legacy—three good-government terms in Albany where, more than anyone else, he has kept alive the flickering fires of Federalism. And he leaves, too, that 1966 campaign. It is no mean legacy.

That he won the campaign is astounding.

Briefly, let's go back in time, to set the scene. In 1964, Rockefeller worked hard to win the presidential nomination. Buffeted by what his advisers call the "personal problem"—his divorce and subsequent remarriage to a younger woman—he doggedly wooed the voters in New Hampshire and Oregon and California. He spent millions in what a reasonable man could have told him was a futile struggle. It was Nelson Rockefeller who led the attack against Barry Goldwater; Rockefeller first leveled the charges about Goldwater's positions on Social Security, nuclear weapons, the progressive income tax, civil rights. Who can forget Rockefeller trying to talk to the Republican National Convention in San Francisco's smoky, cavernous Cow Palace? Who can forget the anger, the frustration, and the rudeness of those delegates who interrupted his almost every word with rolling waves of derision?

Rockefeller returned to New York a beaten man who had won the everlasting enmity of the most vocal minority within his own party. But Rockefeller is stubborn; some use another word—arrogant. It is hard for a Rockefeller to believe he can't triumph over adversity.

No sooner had 1965 begun than Rockefeller began planning for his reelection campaign in 1966. His chief adviser was heavy-set William J. Ronan, onetime dean of the New York University School of Public Administration and

Social Services.* Mr. Ronan—Dr. Ronan really—is an issues man and no friend of New York's old-fashioned political leaders. Ronan, the bosses tell you, is a thinker; you don't win elections with intellectuals. As usual—as happened in Pennsylvania and Michigan and even Arkansas—the politicians were wrong. Dr. Ronan planned the Rockefeller campaign; more than any other technician, he won the campaign.

"We had a problem," Dr. Ronan recalls, in a nice piece of understatement. "In January of 1966 the position of the governor in the polls was not very good. Indications were that almost anyone could beat him. There were so many negatives. He had been in office for almost eight years and he had made a lot of decisions that irritated some people; some other people just thought they were aggrieved. He'd raised taxes twice in a major way. One was a permanent sales tax. And he got full credit for all these new taxes." Another point Ronan overlooks: In 1962 Rockefeller promised he would impose no new taxes; once elected, he pushed through a program of higher "fees." Most people in New York saw little difference between higher "fees" and higher taxes.

"Then," Ronan continues, "he had this very long session with the Legislature and a struggle over Medicaid [New York's program that takes over where Federal medicare leaves off]. The compromise was higher than the original bill, and the governor got credit for that. It was only after the bill was passed that newspapers pointed out its cost to state and local government. The result was a furor in the Buffalo and Syracuse areas.

"So you had taxes, Medicaid, eight years in office. Also, there was the so-called personal problem. Some people al-

---

* Money does count. Romney has been able to recruit young professors. Rockefeller hires *deans*.

leged it was still there." Again, a reference to Rockefeller's divorce and remarriage.

"Then, on the other side, Rockefeller had accomplished much more in eight years than any other governor. But these positives weren't apparent. He'd done so much it was all kind of a blur—the state university, highways, aid to local government, health, parks, right across the board. I could sense it at cocktail parties. People were all criticizing the governor. So we'd say, 'What about the state university?' And they'd say, 'What?' It was clear there was no public understanding of his actual accomplishments. Adding it all up, the governor just wasn't popular. People didn't like him anymore."

The situation was so bad, in fact, that some Republican leaders actually were calling upon Rockefeller to step down in favor of United States Senator Jacob K. Javits. Some of Rockefeller's own staffers were morosely hinting that defeat was inevitable. But things weren't quite so bad as they seemed. "Fortune favors the brave," Ronan notes.

One of the secrets of Rockefeller's campaign success—a secret, as we have seen, that's shared by others—was its early start. First, there was Dr. Ronan, ready to go on issues. Then, there was the "other Bill"—William L. Pfeiffer, a salty professional who had worked for Rockefeller before. For the 1966 campaign, he actually went on the payroll on December 1, 1964. His assignment was to organize the 1966 campaign—to pick the personnel, to open the headquarters, to lay out a schedule. Bill Ronan was the ideas man; Bill Pfeiffer was the organization man. Ultimately, Pfeiffer put together a *paid* staff of 307 people, 190 of them working out of headquarters at the New York Hilton. In a more traditional way, Pfeiffer's operation was as brilliant as Ronan's, as we shall see a bit later.

Yet, with all credit to Pfeiffer's operation, the major assignment was Ronan's. He had to *sell* Rockefeller; he had to make the governor credible again. And he had so very far to go.

Ronan put together a small organization of three or four men and one woman, himself at its head, that he called, grandiloquently, the Substantive Issues Group.

"We had to devise a strategy to overcome the governor's disabilities," Ronan says. "Because the routine of day-to-day public relations apparently had been unsuccessful, we had, first of all, to tell the people what had been accomplished. I wanted to find a series of methods to show what had been done. This, I felt, was one way of overcoming the disability of the higher taxes. I thought people would accept the taxes if they could see what had been done with the money. This is not an easy sort of thing to do, and there were people who said it couldn't be done. Some people in our own camp said you couldn't change how people felt about the governor by doing this sort of thing. After everything was done, they said, people still wouldn't like the governor. I felt differently, and so did some others.

"So we undertook a precampaign approach. We wanted to improve the governor's position before the state convention [the ticket in New York was then chosen by party convention, not by a primary election]. Since people were down on the governor, we decided to sell his accomplishments without using him at all."

This kind of project—an organized precampaign build-up—is as far as I know singular. It was also very expensive. Its success depended in large measure upon the material that would be developed to refurbish the governor. Thus, a key decision was the choice of an advertising agency.

"We wanted to depart from the usual political approach," Ronan says. "So we moseyed around the field and we found Jack Tinker & Partners, part of the Interpublic complex. We liked their different approach. It was offbeat and it had been successful in restoring some products." One of those "restored" products was Alka-Seltzer (through commercials showing, one after another, people's stomachs at work and at play). Another was Braniff Airways, Inc. (through a campaign in which the airplanes were painted wild colors and the stewardesses dressed in exotic clothes).

Ronan is a meticulous man who works in a meticulous office. The Tinker offices, in 1966, were something less than businesslike in appearance. The visitor walked from the corridor into a large, comfortable living room, with a fireplace and a well-stocked bar, couches, cushioned chairs, and brigades of miniskirted girls dashing breathlessly through the clutter, hands clutching mugs of coffee. This is the place where the celebrated Mary Wells worked until she defected to open her own agency. It was Mary Wells, in fact, who made the presentation to the Rockefeller staffers that won the day; she left the agency only days later.

But, with or without Mary Wells, the Tinker agency has a flair and a style about it that's quite remarkable. The favorite word of the people who work there is *creative*. The trademark of any Tinker commercial—Rockefeller, Carling beer, Alka-Seltzer—is its rapport with the person who is going to be looking at it. Says Jack Conroy, who supervised the Rockefeller account: "Each of our commercials tries to talk with the viewer. You talk to the people in front of their sets in their own terms. This is almost automatic with the Tinker people."

The Tinker agency had never worked for a political client before. And no politician had ever hired an agency quite like Tinker. The agreement between Rockefeller and

Tinker was reached about the first of April, fully five months before the Republican State Convention was scheduled to convene in September. Ronan had hoped that the first commercials would be ready to go by July. But these things take time; the commercials weren't ready until early August.

The Tinker people still remember their first meeting with Governor Rockefeller and his staff. "The meeting was in the governor's private office on Fifty-fifth Street," a Tinker partner says. "The governor was there and so was Ronan, and the governor's private pollsters were there too. We were impressed by the governor's evaluation of his problems. And I remember one of the pollsters got up and said, 'You couldn't be elected dogcatcher.' " *

Without sufficient time, Rockefeller couldn't have won. Time, in the new politics, is always a necessity. Because Rockefeller was an incumbent, and because he was far-sighted, he had the time to prepare his campaign. His Democratic opponent, Frank D. O'Connor, didn't have the time—or didn't take advantage of what time he did have—and he lost.

"Advance planning is so damn important," Tinker's Jack Conroy says. "I don't see why a lot of incumbents don't start planning a lot sooner. And, in fact, I don't see why the out-party couldn't start early too. The state committee could put together a program attacking the incumbent and his record, even without having a candidate of its own."

---

* Rockefeller owns that five-story building on Fifty-fifth Street, and uses it as his New York City state house. A passageway connects the building to another nearby where the Rockefellers maintain their own private dining room. Rockefeller's pollsters are "private" too: their identity has long been carefully guarded. The chief pollster is, in fact, Lloyd A. Free, a long-time personal friend. Free works for Rockefeller in conjunction with that veteran pollster Archibald Crossley. Together, they write the interviews and analyze the results. The Gallup organization handles the coding and computer runs.

And so the work began. Polls helped to pick out the relevant issues. Ronan and his staff talked to the Tinker people about ways those issues might be illustrated in commercials. "Finally," says Ronan, "we settled on those issues that directly affect the lives of people—highways, higher education, local schools, health, the minimum wage, pollution." Ronan and his team had the final word on what issues would be stressed; it was Tinker's job to illuminate those issues.

Bill Pfeiffer describes the problem: "It was tricky. We had to sell the record, associate it with the governor. And it had to be done so subtly it crept up on you before you knew what the hell had happened to you."

Tinker commercials are prepared by teams. Each team is composed of a copywriter and an art director. Unlike most agencies, the two members of a Tinker team follow the commercial all the way through the production process, from writing the script to directing the filming to editing the sound. Two of these teams were assigned to the Rockefeller account. Working on the Number One team were Eugene Case, writer, and Bob Reitzfeld, art director. After the election, Reitzfeld defected to Mary Wells's agency. Working on the Number Two team were Jim Symon, writer, and Julio DiOrio, art director.

The first commercials produced by these Tinker teams were all sixty seconds in length. Each was done in a process called sound-on-film; it's slower to produce but the quality is better. Moreover, a creative team can do more with film than with tape. It is not surprising that most of the Rockefeller commercials were sound-on-film; that all of the Democratic commercials were videotape.

Says Jack Conroy: "If you get together after the convention to select an agency and to get going, and only then decide your issues and subjects, then it would probably be late September before you had anything to show. That means you have only six or eight weeks left to the election. When you're that late, there's a reluctance to spend much money on production; you just want to get on the air. This is why so many political commercials are taped; it's faster and cheaper."

The first Tinker commercial set the tone of the early phase of the campaign. The title of the commercial was "Fish Interview." Here is the actual script for both video and audio:

VIDEO	AUDIO
1. *Open on hand wearing a press hat and microphone to resemble a reporter talking to a fish puppet. Super for first :05: simulated interview with large-mouth bass.*	1. REPORTER: You, sir . . .
2. *Fish reacts.*	2. FISH: Uh huh . . .
3.	3. REPORTER: How do you feel about Governor Rockefeller's Pure Waters Program?
4.	4. FISH: His pure what?
5.	5. REPORTER: Pure Waters . . .
6.	6. FISH: Oh, Oh, yeah . . .
7.	7. REPORTER: This program, sir, is wiping out water pollution in New York State within six years.
8.	8. FISH: Wait a minute! *He's* supposed to be interviewing *me*.
9.	9. REPORTER: Already, 130

10.

11.

12. *Fish does quick imitation of death of his cousin. Gasps, wriggles, and sinks out of frame. Then swims back up to reporter.*

13.

14.

15.

16. *Whispers into reporter's ear.*
Super:
A paid political announcement by Friends of the Rockefeller Team.

new sewage-treatment plants are getting under way.

10. FISH: Well, it *was* pretty smelly down here. . . .

11. REPORTER: State health officers are working overtime, tracking down sources of pollution.

12. FISH: Listen, they should see what happened to my cousin. Ah, oh (*gurgling sounds*). My cousin had a brilliant career.

13. REPORTER: By the end of summer, the Governor will have called in every major pollutor for a hearing.

14. FISH: I would say, uh, next to a fish . . . I'd say he's the best Gov . . .

15. REPORTER: Already, over 70 cities and industries have agreed to correct violations.

16. FISH: (*brief pause*): Frankly, my problem with Rockefeller is, some of his best friends are fishermen.

Bill Pfeiffer remembers looking at the first Tinker commercials, such as this one, with a number of old party leaders. "The politicos said it was no damn good. They're so used to the staged stuff, to the candidate standing there talking. You had to wait out these Tinker commercials to find out what they were all about. The politicos thought they were just a waste of time. That's when I knew we had done the right thing."

Each commercial dealt with a single subject, directly and imaginatively. And, sometimes, they were almost as funny as they were supposed to be.

The second Tinker commercial was classic in its simplicity. That commercial was called "Road to Hawaii." Here is the script:

VIDEO	AUDIO
1. *A stretch of road, as viewed from camera mounted on hood of car. Dotted white lines whip by.*	1. *(Road sounds)*
2. *Road whips by.*	2. *(Road sounds under)*— ANNCR *(Voice off)*: If you took all the roads Governor Rockefeller has built, and all the roads he's widened and straightened and smoothed out . . . , if you took all these roads, and laid them end to end, they'd stretch all the way to . . . Hawaii.
3. *Car stops abruptly, covering road ahead, sand.*	3. *(Sound of breakers and Hawaiian music)*
4. *Car backs up, swings around and proceeds forward.*	4. All the way to Hawaii . . .
5. *Remainder of commercial same road is seen, same dotted white line whips by.*	5. . . . and all the way back. *(Road sounds up)*
6. *Super:* A paid political announcement by Friends of the Rockefeller Team.	

Most of these commercials were reproduced for radio. It often requires very little change. Here, for example, is the "Road to Hawaii" *radio* script (SFX means sound effects):

SFX: *(Road sounds of car moving at 50–60 mph)*
ANNCR: *(Road sounds under)*: If you took all the roads Governor Rockefeller has built, and all the roads Governor Rockefeller has widened, and all the roads he's straightened and smoothed out—if you took all those roads, and laid them end to end, they'd stretch all the way to Hawaii.
SFX: *Hear car stopping. Then Hawaiian hula music and surf. Hear car back away from music, shift gears and hear it head back down road.*
ANNCR: *(Road sounds under, with car picking up speed)* All the way to Hawaii, and all the way back.
2ND ANNCR: A paid political announcement by Friends of the Rockefeller Team.

"Butterfingers," the third television commercial in this precampaign series, is my personal favorite. Here, as the last full example we'll show, is that script:

VIDEO	AUDIO
1. *Open on full shot of kid approaching camera dribbling basketball. Cuts of a pickup basketball game in a lower-class neighborhood. There are about five tall, fast, good ballplayers and one short, fat inept kid.*	1. *(Music)*
2. *The camera from time to time draws the viewers' attention to the inept kid. He is the one the message is addressed to.*	2. *(Music under)* ANNCR *(Voice off)*: Hey kid. Want to go to college? Maybe you catch the eye of some coach, get yourself a scholarship. No, you don't have

to be nine feet tall to get a scholarship, or a blooming genius either. Why, if you can get *into* college, you can get the money to help you *go* to college. From New York State. Two hundred thousand new state scholarships and grants are sitting there waiting, every year. Two hundred thousand new chances to make it, every year, even for you, shorty . . . tubby . . . butterfingers. The man who did it, the man responsible for those new scholarships is Governor Rockefeller. Who was no Bob Cousy himself.

3. *Super:*
A paid political announcement by Friends of the Rockefeller Team.

Governor Rockefeller appeared in none of these early commercials. His voice wasn't even used.* The Tinker agency picked a professional—actor Ed Binns—to read the scripts. It was this same Binns, you may remember, who recorded the

---

* Thought, however, was given to "warming up" the governor's image. "Under pressure," reports Tinker's Myron McDonald, "we did make a fifteen-minute film of the governor called 'Governor Rockefeller, The Man.' We sent a crew of people up to the 'Camp,' as it is called, in Maine, which had the governor and little Nelson and Mrs. Rockefeller for a week of 'roughing it.' I put our people under strict orders to take the worst possible pictures of this operation. I'd never seen the Camp. They came back and the worst possible pictures they could take of the Camp came out looking like the Orangerie at Versailles. We did not use the fifteen-minute film."

Milton Shapp radio commercials in Pennsylvania's general election. Binns is even better known as the voice behind the Alka-Seltzer and Gillette razor commercials.

A few of the commercials got on the air in late July; most began running in early August. All of them were scheduled scientifically, based on market research of the potential *political* audience.

The Rockefeller people had isolated their own version of "heavyweight" counties. They had found that 86.7 percent of the state's registered voters lived in just 22 of the state's 62 counties. Thus, these 60-second commercials were scheduled for the six stations in New York City and for stations serving Albany, Binghamton, Buffalo, Rochester, and Syracuse.

The television campaign was divided into three phases. Phase 1 covered the period from July 5 to September 12. During those weeks, the schedule called for running 37 Rockefeller 60-second commercials every week in New York City and 18 every week in each of the five upstate markets. The result was that these precampaign commercials—stressing the administration's accomplishments but never once picturing the governor himself—were shown 700 times before the convention in September even opened.

Because of the nature of this campaign—its soft-sell emphasis—hardly any prime-time television was purchased. Most of the commercials were run during the daytime or early or very late evening.

This, of course, was only part of the preconvention strategy. The governor himself quietly toured the state all during August, shaking hands and trying to make friends. Personal emissaries—men like the gentle but persuasive George Hinman—toured the state, talking to "opinion makers." An indication of the success of this effort may be the fact that only two daily newspapers in the state—the *Adirondack Enterprise* and the Syracuse *Herald-Journal*—ultimately decided to support a candidate opposed to Rockefeller. In New York City, both the liberal *Post* and the conservative *Daily News* endorsed Rockefeller.*

Dr. Ronan and his Substantive Issues Group were busy with other things too. One of these projects was campaign literature. "We had long felt most of it is not very valid," Dr. Ronan says. "There's a picture of a guy and it says, 'Vote for Joe Smith.' Now, here we had Nelson Rockefeller, one of the most visible of people. He'd run twice in the state and tried for President twice. He was ubiquitous. There was no need to try to produce a recognition factor. Just what we didn't want people saying was, 'Aha, there's Nelson Rockefeller.' "

And so much of the Rockefeller literature turned out to be striking and original too.

"First," says Dr. Ronan, "we wanted to reach the opinion makers, for we were afraid we had lost them. They just weren't articulate for us, and I mean the legislators, the newspaper people, the leaders of various special groups. So we decided to approach them on a clientele basis. We prepared eye-getting stuff in each category—a brochure for the people in the field of mental retardation, another for labor, another for fine arts." Bill Pfeiffer puts it in somewhat more pungent terms: "It was out of this world. We had something for every group except the Times Square prostitutes."

Joe Napolitan had some pretty fair literature too. As we saw, however, he wasn't sure it ever was distributed properly.

---

* Which is roughly parallel to the situation of the liberal Nashville *Tennesseean* and the very conservative Nashville *Banner* in 1964; both were supporting Republican Howard Baker for the Senate. The editor of the *Tennesseean* called the editor of the *Banner*. "One of us," he said, "must be wrong."

In this Rockefeller campaign, a paid worker was assigned to each kind of brochure with instructions to make sure the literature got to the people for whom it had been written. Thus, if there was a meeting anywhere in the state attended by people interested in higher education, there was a Rockefeller staffer on hand to make sure everyone got a brochure detailing what the governor claimed to have done for higher education.

Another Ronan innovation was the preparation of a series of brochures aimed at individual regions in the state. Every major region had a Rockefeller brochure, and the text in each told precisely what the governor had done for that part of the state. Getting the appropriate facts out of the bureaucracy was the tough part of that job; it was accomplished only because the pressure was applied early.

Beyond this, the Ronan group prepared immense research reports for each of the state's sixty-two counties. These data sheets showed how many miles of highway had been built, and where; the number of new bridges; the number of state scholarships awarded to county students; even specific examples showing what property taxes would have been had it not been for expanded state aid. All the candidates used these data sheets in their personal campaigning.

A bulkier document was called "The Massive Record." It was a salubrious account of the accomplishments of the Rockefeller administration and it was distributed to all the candidates and all the campaign workers. A shorter version, "The Massive Rockefeller Record: A Ruthlessly Condensed Version," was prepared for ordinary voters. Its introduction gives some idea of the flavor:

> Why a ruthlessly condensed version? No booklet could give you the full detail of the Governor's record. In a word, the record is massive. The man has simply done so much that a

full listing of his achievements would fill volumes and you'd
still be reading when the election is over. And so the record
has been cut, sliced, and chopped—ruthlessly—into this easy-
reading booklet, which we hope will give you some measure of
what Governor Rockefeller has accomplished during his eight
years in office.

Clem Whitaker wasn't the last to wield a heavy ladle.

Because they had started so early, the Rockefeller people
had time to anticipate the issues. Polls were taken regularly.
They showed that one of the major criticisms of the governor was that he was arrogant. "So," says Dr. Ronan, "we
flipped that over to the positive. The positive of arrogance
is leadership. We said, 'This is leadership and let's keep it
in Albany.' It came through again and again in what we did.
It was summed up by the phrase, 'He Cares.' "

The polls continued to show that people were still angry
about high taxes. The reaction to that was a continuing effort
to show what the money had bought. Special emphasis was
placed on the amount of tax money that had been returned
to local jurisdictions in the form of state aid. The issue, some
suspect, was never overcome; it was, however, blunted.

The Rockefeller people also tried to anticipate their
opponent. They guessed right that Frank D. O'Connor, president of the New York City Council, would be the Democrats'
choice. O'Connor, probably as part of a package deal, was
chosen at the Democratic State Convention in Buffalo on
September 7–8. By then, the Republicans had a fat file on his
career and almost everything he had ever said.

Frank O'Connor is one of the most charming politicians
I have ever met. He's one of those Irishmen who simply refuses to take life terribly seriously; he laughs at himself and
everyone around him, and accepts life for what it is—whimsi-
cal.

On the face of it, though, one would be hard put to find a more typical representative of old-fashioned, big-city politics. O'Connor's mother came from County Limerick, his father from County Sligo. O'Connor himself has lived all but three years of his life amid unpretentious surroundings in the Borough of Queens. As a young man, he joined the local Democratic club. He went to law school, opened a practice in Queens, and voted the straight ticket. Party regularity then—and even today—has special rewards. O'Connor's first reward was his selection by party leaders in 1948 as their candidate for the state Senate. In Albany, O'Connor was a party loyalist. And some of the bills he introduced were— in the light of later events—ill-advised. In one resolution, he called for an end of Marshall Plan aid to Great Britain because the British had recognized Red China. In another, he urged a plebiscite to reunite Ireland. The ones that really came back to haunt him, however, were bills that smacked of McCarthyism. In one of these bills, he sought to establish a two-year residency requirement for welfare recipients. In another, he sought a loyalty oath for schoolteachers. In still another, he sought mandatory pledges of allegiance in all the state's public schools.

Just before he was chosen to run for governor, I asked him about those old bills. "That all happened," he said, "when I was young and foolish. They raise those old bills every time I run. I don't blame them. I'd do just the same."

O'Connor continued to move up through the party chairs. From the Senate, he moved on to become district attorney of Queens, where he remained for ten long and generally uneventful years. He played the game according to all the rules. His assistant district attorneys were party regulars too, all of them recommended by their leaders. And all of them were allowed to maintain their own private practices.

In 1962 O'Connor made a stab at the gubernatorial nomination. At the last minute, though, party leaders pushed through a name no one had even thought about—Robert Morgenthau, son of FDR's secretary of the Treasury and United States attorney in New York. Polls supposedly had showed that a Jew with a Roosevelt miasma would do well. Morgenthau was simply chewed up by Rockefeller.

In 1965 O'Connor considered running for mayor. But, in a subterranean party decision, he was told to stand aside and wait for the gubernatorial nomination in 1966. He acceded to the wishes of party leaders and ran for president of the City Council. He was easily elected at the same time that Republican John Lindsay was being elected mayor, and O'Connor outpolled everyone by 200,000 votes.

By 1966 O'Connor had abandoned most of the "foolish" ways of his youth. He was on record as an ardent supporter of civil rights; he favored the controversial police civilian review board; he wanted children bussed from one school to another to overcome de facto segregation. And he was the only district attorney in the state to oppose capital punishment.

It did him no good; New York's rigid, unbending liberals would not accept him. "There is a strange suspicion among [liberals] and reformers concerning an Irishman," O'Connor said in another of those moments of candor. "And to have been an Irish-Catholic DA—no matter what your record, no matter what your promises—it's hard to convince them that you're a liberal." His critics jumped on him for raising the "religious issue," but he had a solid point.

The choice of O'Connor—and the distrust he inspired among liberals—was Nelson Rockefeller's luckiest break. Luckier than it would have been in other states, for in New York some liberals belong to a capital-L Liberal Party. For a number of reasons, some of them unworthy, the Liberal Party would not go along with O'Connor, as they had always gone along with Democratic candidates for governor in the past. The Liberals finally selected, of all people, Franklin Delano Roosevelt, Jr., as their candidate for governor. "Young" Roosevelt, of course, was the same fellow who had once worked for Trujillo, who called Hubert Humphrey a draft dodger in West Virginia, and who was elected to Congress in 1949 as the candidate of the Liberal Party, only to turn on his old friends two years later.

At the time all this was happening, I talked with the Reverend Donald S. Harrington, pastor of Park Avenue's Community Church and chairman of the Liberal Party. "I have no illusions about Frank Roosevelt's shortcomings," he told me. "Some of his past is unsavory. But I am firmly convinced that this is a new Roosevelt. He spent a whole afternoon with me right here in this office three weeks ago. And I can tell you he impressed me with his desire to present a new face and to be a new person. He is in his fifties now, and I am convinced he wants to live up to what his name stands for. He wishes to find a place for himself; he wants to redeem himself. He is absolutely tenacious about this."

It is hardly any wonder that Frank O'Connor finds life hard to take seriously. A Roosevelt, he found, can be redeemed; an O'Connor cannot.

The Democrats, however, weren't wholly innocent. Party leaders for years have resented the imperious ways of the Liberals. This time, many of them thought, they could win without the Liberals. In fact, they *wanted* to show they could go it alone. After all, these bosses would tell you, didn't the polls show anyone could beat Rockefeller?

Early polls showed just that, but early polls had showed too that Morganthau would be a strong candidate. What happened was that the Democrats committed one of the most fundamental errors in the new politics; they transferred the findings of a preliminary poll to the outcome of the election itself. Having done so, they relaxed.

The Roosevelt candidacy on the Liberal line wasn't the only splinter. Just as the Liberals are ideologues on the left, so is the new Conservative Party on the right. It was the Conservatives who played fun and games in 1965 by running gadfly William F. Buckley, Jr., for mayor. In 1965 the Conservatives refused to stomach John Lindsay, one of the new nonideological "problem-solvers." In 1966 they faced their *bete noir,* Nelson A. Rockefeller, the man who destroyed Barry Goldwater. So the Conservatives chose as their candidate Paul L. Adams, a professor at an anonymous little upstate college. And the Conservatives had an issue—the referendum testing New York City's civilian review board. The Conservatives were alone in pushing the referendum to upset the board; polls showed that hundreds of thousands of New Yorkers, a great many of them Democrats, supported the Conservative Party's position.

Thus, for poor Frank O'Connor, thunder on both the left and the right. And, for Nelson Rockefeller, the lucky break he needed.

The Rockefeller organization shifted easily from its pre-convention campaign to its actual election campaign. It had all been carefully planned, and hardly any changes were required. Gradually, radio and television began to zero in on O'Connor. Finally, in the last few days, Rockefeller himself came on camera to attack with extraordinary vehemence his bumbling and gentle opponent.

It is almost inconceivable—but true—that the Democratic organization was unable to make any meaningful reply. O'Connor's campaign was pathetically inept. Chartered planes and buses somehow disappeared. At least one advance man got lost. Press releases never got written. Staffers couldn't find petty cash to pay for the simplest kinds of trips.

For at least a year, O'Connor had known he would be the Democratic candidate for governor and that his opponent would be Rockefeller. But he had done nothing about planning a campaign. His own staff was small and amateurish, and terribly self-centered. When O'Connor won the nomination, some old hands were sent in to help by Senator Robert F. Kennedy. Stephen E. Smith, a Kennedy brother-in-law, actually became campaign manager. And a political management firm, U.S. R&D, headed by William Haddad and Robert Clampitt, moved into the seedy headquarters in the Commodore Hotel. But the two factions—the old O'Connor workers and the new Kennedy team—spent as much time feuding with each other as they did plotting strategy against Rockefeller.

Television was produced for O'Connor, but it was ineffectual and some of it wasn't even usable. One whole day, for example, was used to film O'Connor discussing urban problems in a tenement district. O'Connor spoke posed against a doorway. When the film was produced and viewed for the first time, a young female staffer spotted what everyone else had missed—the graffiti scrawled on the doorway.

Meanwhile, the Tinker agency had returned to Rockefeller's battle, preparing ten- and twenty-second commercials attacking O'Connor and his record. Typical was this script: "Frank O'Connor, the man who led the fight against the New York State Thruway [as a state senator], is running for governor. Get in your car. Drive down to the polls, and vote."

Of necessity, all spot commercials are oversimplifications. No one can say very much in sixty seconds, and hardly anything in ten. The precampaign Rockefeller commercials, however, were ethically acceptable, given the limitations of the medium. Each of those commercials was sixty seconds, and each made a point that had some validity.

But, in these final phases of the campaign, Rockefeller's commercials took a very sharp turn for the worse. Take that Thruway commercial. O'Connor, as a state legislator, didn't actually oppose a thruway. What he did oppose—taking his usual cue from the Democratic leadership—was a toll road. He and the Democrats wanted a free highway; it was the Republicans that wanted the highway users to pay for the road. The refinements, naturally enough, were never explained, because Rockefeller didn't want to explain, and O'Connor didn't have a chance.

Or take another example, this time a twenty-second commercial. The script reads: "Frank O'Connor from New York City is running for governor. He says the subways should be free. Guess who he thinks should be paying for them?" It is interesting that this commercial ran only in *upstate* New York. Moreover, it badly garbles O'Connor's real position. He had never made a specific proposal to eliminate fares on New York subway lines; he had only been musing about long-term possibilities and he had been thinking about subway lines in all cities. Again, his organization was never able to explain the subtleties.

In every hard-fought campaign, smart politicians look for the "gut issue"—an emotional, supercharged (and usually transient) issue that can be battered home to every voter. The Rockefeller people, months before the campaign began, had anticipated such an issue. When the time came to pull the trigger, they were ready.

The issue, specifically, was narcotics; more broadly, it was crime, which, as we have seen, was the prime issue in 1966 in most big states and cities. As part of his legislative package, Rockefeller had proposed a wide-ranging narcotics program in which pushers were to be relentlessly hunted down and jailed and addicts were to be swept off the streets and given mandatory treatment. It was strong stuff, so strong that it worried many civil libertarians. Yet, for voters generally, it was popular enough. In 1966 any proposal that seemed to come to grips with the crime problem found ready acceptance.

From some of O'Connor's earlier statements, the Rockefeller people expected he would take a position against the Rockefeller narcotics program. So they baited the trap, and waited. O'Connor took the bait—he came out foursquare against the Rockefeller program. The Rockefeller people slammed the trap shut.

Some people say O'Connor came out against the program in the hope that his position would win back some liberal Democrats who were flocking to Frank Roosevelt and the Liberal Party. O'Connor himself says he opposed the program because he simply felt it was a bad program and should be opposed.

Either way, O'Connor was vulnerable, and he was clobbered by every device available to the opposition. The television commercials were eerie, frightening. A police car, lights flashing, cruises down a dark street. There's the sound of footsteps in the background. A disembodied voice begins talking: "If you walk home at night or if there's a teen-ager in your family, you should be worried. Governor Rockefeller's worried. As much as half the crime in New York is caused by addicts. That's why the governor has sponsored a tough new law that can get addicts off the street for up to three years. . . ."

At first, these commercials—produced again by Tinker—made no mention of O'Connor. But then they began to draw him into the web. As district attorney of Queens, one said, he had been alone among all prosecutors in opposing a tough narcotics law. Finally, Rockefeller himself took the fight directly to his opponent. He filmed a number of hard-hitting commercials in a studio, a battery of microphones in front of him, and a claque seated in his audience. "If you want to keep the crime rates high," he concluded one of these commercials, "O'Connor is your man." That's a long way from "Butterfingers" and "Road to Hawaii."

It was devastating, and it was heightened by the inability of the O'Connor organization to make a significant reply. Its impact was deepened, too, because of that referendum in New York City dealing with the police civilian review board. It is also my opinion that the Rockefeller people, *perhaps* unintentionally, used this issue to play upon the white backlash. As Fred Currier has noted, the civil-rights issue takes all kinds of turns in which code words become important signals. "Crime on the streets" is surely one of these. The Rockefeller people emphatically deny they intended to work over this kind of ground. But I think they did.

While Ronan and his group were orchestrating the issues, Bill Pfeiffer and his people were putting together an organization. That organization was interesting enough to deserve some description.

Party organization in a state as large and as old as New York is, at least on paper, cumbersome. There are, in each party, sixty-two county chairmen and vice-chairmen and a grand total of 22,000 committeemen and committeewomen. "So," says Pfeiffer, "we divided the state into seven areas for easier communication. Each of these seven areas had a chairman and a vice-chairman and they all worked full time, seven days a week, days and nights, for three months."

These regional chairmen were in daily contact with their county leaders, and every day they had to report to headquarters in New York. "This way," says Pfeiffer, "we could detect weaknesses. And when we detected weaknesses we sent out shock troops from New York to set things right. That kept them on their toes."

All the campaigns—from governor on down to the state legislature and delegates to the Constitutional Convention— were run out of the Hilton Hotel headquarters. That, too, is where the checks were written.

The operation in New York City was actually separate from the rest of the organization. The city had its own boss, Jack Wells, an old Rockefeller hand. And he and his people borrowed heavily from the 1965 Lindsay campaign. Once again, storefront headquarters were opened in the heart of Democratic districts to show the flag and prove that Republicans don't necessarily wear horns. Wells opened some thirty storefronts, less than one-quarter the number Lindsay opened.

But the Rockefeller organization did come up with a gimmick—mobile storefronts. These were converted Dodge campers that were wired for sound and had radio communication with headquarters. "We manned them," says Pfeiffer, "with attractive men and women. We did the speaking from the roofs and distributed literature from the open sides. We followed the crowds all over the city. If we saw Macy's was going to have a sale, we'd know damn well women would be jammed around the store an hour before opening. So we'd be there. We had ten of these campers working the city and six more upstate. They were going all day long every day, and they attracted a lot of attention."

Each camper and each storefront was manned by at least one paid member of the Rockefeller staff. "Volunteers are well meaning," says Pfeiffer, "but you need five or ten of them to do the work of one paid full-timer."

Pfeiffer had 190 people on the payroll at the Hilton and

another 118 on the payroll upstate. If the average weekly paycheck was $200 (perhaps high) and if the average length of time on the payroll was 14 weeks, that bill comes to about $900,000 Rockefeller money.

It is worth noting here that the 1966 organization in New York was a Rockefeller organization; there was no Republican organization as such, except on paper. The same thing happened in Michigan; that was a Romney organization. In Pennsylvania, Milton Shapp clobbered the Democratic organization in the primary and then pretty much built his own for the general election.

There has to be an explanation for this—and it's an obvious one: Successful politicians often don't need the party organization because it's too weak and too hidebound. It's usually easier to build a one-shot organization around the principal candidate. In Michigan, Romney for the first time in his life really gave a hand to the rest of his ticket. In New York, Rockefeller did what he could, which wasn't very much. He won, but almost everyone else lost. In 1964, Democrats turned out seven Republican congressmen. In 1966, the Democrats held on to every one of those seats. As a *party* leader, Rockefeller was a failure in 1966.

Rockefeller spent a great deal of money to win reelection in 1966. How much?

During the campaign, Eugene H. Nickerson, Nassau County executive [roughly comparable to mayor] and an early contender for the Democratic nomination for governor, said Rockefeller was trying to buy the election with $20,-000,000. Carl Spad, the Republican state chairman, rebutted the charge with a wonderfully innocent statement. "For example," he said, "they [the Democrats] have been screaming that we've bought up all the billboard space in the state. This is a complete falsehood. Our [advertising] agency has recommended against the use of billboards and, to date, we have contracted for absolutely none whatever."

The official figure filed by the Rockefeller committees was $4,800,000. "I spent every nickel that was spent," says Bill Pfeiffer, "and that's it. We wouldn't in the slightest deviate from the law. The Rockefeller family is one of the most important in the world. They're not going to be caught on that sort of thing."

Pfeiffer is an honest and honorable man, and I'm sure he saw to it that the law was strictly complied with. But the law, in campaign financing, is an uncertain thing. My own study of campaign costs in New York would indicate a figure somewhere closer to $6,000,000, of which most came from members of the Rockefeller family or their friends. "It's nice," as Pfeiffer says, "to have a lot of brothers and aunts and uncles."

At least $2,000,000 of this total was spent for television. Consider some of these figures:

On television station WNBC, in New York City, the Rockefeller organization ran 208 commercials. They paid $237,000 in air time to do it. The O'Connor organization ran 23 commercials on this same station, and paid $41,000. On WCBS, Rockefeller outspent O'Connor $231,105 to $35,920. On WABC, the third network station in the city, it was $137,000 for Rockefeller and $25,100 for O'Connor.

The disparity upstate was sometimes even more striking. On WBEN in Buffalo, Rockefeller spent $27,762; O'Connor spent $2,465. Little WWNY in Watertown ran 99 Rockefeller commercials, for $3,067.50, against 18 O'Connor commercials, at $1,307.50.

Rockefeller strategists hasten to point out that they began their television campaign in late July. And of course that's right—but they had to start that early to win. The early spending was just as crucial as the final spending. It was, in fact, one campaign. And when it was all over Rockefeller outspent O'Connor about 6 to 1.

Even with this lopsided spending, Rockefeller didn't win by much. The final count was: Rockefeller, 2,690,626; O'Connor, 2,298,363; Adams (the Conservative), 510,023; and Roosevelt (the Liberal), 507,234.

The figures show that Rockefeller could have been beaten; he *should* have been beaten. He won only because he had so much money, so much talent working for him—and, finally, a bit of luck.

Perhaps more than any other campaign we have examined, the Rockefeller campaign suggests some patterns for the future. Among them:

1. The need for money, and more money. Money wisely, even ruthlessly, spent. A candidate or a party must have it early and spend it often.

2. Television. It is ordinarily the premier instrument for political campaigning. It penetrates into almost every home; it sways and angers and even converts. Item: During the week of October 18, Rockefeller ran 74 television commercials in New York City. They were seen in 91 percent of all television homes in the city (and 5,600,000 of 6,000,000 New York homes have television). Not just seen once in each home, either—but seen an average of 9.8 times.

3. Experts. No one wins any more with amateurs. Good television means people like Dr. Ronan and the copywriters and art directors at Jack Tinker. Good organization requires professionals like Bill Pfeiffer.

4. Time. It takes time to put together a new-style campaign. Mr. Rockefeller had the time; Mr. O'Connor didn't. It's almost as simple as that.

Perhaps one more lesson. The need for a candidate. I

refuse to believe that *anyone* can be elected, given money, good television, experts, and time to deploy them. Rockefeller, after all, is a great campaigner, and I believe he has been an exceptionally able governor. There was, in all the confusion and bitterness, a genuine product to be marketed, albeit in a battered and dusty package.

Nelson Rockefeller isn't the only political Rockefeller. His brother, Winthrop, is governor of Arkansas. And Winthrop has been breaking new ground too—with data processing and computers. We will take a look at that important, and perhaps ominous, new technique, and then turn, in our final case study, to John Lindsay's campaign for mayor of New York City in 1965.

6

COMPUTERS
AND DATA PROCESSING:
BEGINNING WITH
WINTHROP ROCKEFELLER

LIKE ANY OTHER ROCKEFELLER, WINTHROP, the governor of Arkansas, travels first class. Even to the point of maintaining, in Room 440 of the Tower Building in downtown Little Rock, an IBM 1401 computer whose attachments include a 1402 reader, a 1403 printer, two 1311 disc drives, a document-roll input, and a document converter. Mr. Rockefeller's aides freely admit that without the computer (and all those exotic spare parts) he would never have been elected governor in 1966. And it was partly because of the computer that he was heavily favored to win reelection in 1968.

As far as I know, Winthrop Rockefeller is the only politician in America who maintains his own private computer expressly for political work and who pays, out of his own pocket, a stable of experts to run it.

But, after all, Winthrop Rockefeller can afford a computer. Some people say he and his four brothers and one sister are each worth $200,000,000. Even for a Rockefeller, however, maintaining a computer is something more than a petty-cash item. Rockefeller leases his computer from IBM; it's my best estimate that the monthly charge is about $7,000. And, late in 1967, he was preparing to move up from a 1401 to an IBM 360 (Model 30), a larger, faster computer that will probably lease for about $10,000 a month.

Electronic data processing (EDP)—which more and more involves the use of high-speed computers—is hardly brand-new in American politics. We have already examined the way the Romney organization uses computers in connection with its polls and voting statistics. The Democratic National Committee began experimenting with data processing as early as 1960; in 1967 the Democrats were using a 1401 and, just like Winthrop Rockefeller, were preparing to switch over to a larger IBM 360. The Republican organization in Dallas, Texas, began using EDP in 1962.

By 1967, however, the pace was suddenly accelerating. New firms were being created to specialize in political data processing. And new ways were being found to use computers in politics.

We shall examine in this chapter the ways in which EDP can be effectively used in politics. And we shall also take a look at some of the bizarre uses to which computers are being put that peripherally involve politics.

The Rockefeller operation in Arkansas is a good place to start. It's probably the best example to date of a statewide EDP system at work. The EDP work that's being done in Arkansas is elemental enough so that it probably could be copied in almost any state, congressional district, or large city. It is, in fact, the kind of nuts-and-bolts operation that could be performed by either of the two political parties nationally—a point that both parties have noted.

An Arkansas Rockefeller is an unlikely phenomenon. But Winthrop Rockefeller is no common-garden Rockefeller. He has always been a bit of a maverick, from the day he dropped out of Yale to pursue his education in the big-city fleshpots. In those bon-vivant days, he scandalized his sober-sided relatives by marrying Bobo Sears, who was hardly a blue-book debutante. It was in 1953, after his divorce, that Winthrop Rockefeller arrived in, of all places, Arkansas, to make a new life. He became a rancher, and soon his cowboy hat and boots became his trademark. He has been pretty much of a solid citizen ever since. And he became an industrial do-gooder as the successful chairman of the Arkansas Industrial Development Commission. He was appointed to that job by Democratic Governor Orval Faubus, a bit of business Faubus may later have lived to regret.

No Rockefeller easily disclaims his Republican inheritance. Rather than work with the Democrats (as most newcomers might have done), Rockefeller resolved to build a Republican Party in solidly Democratic Arkansas. He emphasized the dimensions of his folly by becoming Republican national committeeman in 1961.

Seemingly, there was no end to his folly. In 1964 Rockefeller ran for governor against Faubus, whose own segregationist folly had made Little Rock a household word around the world. Rockefeller didn't win, but he managed to round up a surprising 44 percent of the vote.

Having gone that far, Rockefeller decided to run in earnest in 1966. But, he had found in 1964, a Republican running in a one-party Democratic state like Arkansas faces some very special problems. First of all, he has no established party organization. Second, and maybe even worse, he has no list of names to work with or appeal to. In 1964 Rockefeller really didn't know the names of the voters or where they lived or what they thought. This was because all the usual data—what there was of it—reposed in the county courthouses, and all the courthouses were controlled by Democrats.

Yet, in a haphazard sort of way, Rockefeller—beginning as far back as 1961—had been collecting names. "It was a mound of information," says Marion B. Burton, Rockefeller's executive secretary and the man who ultimately took charge of the EDP program. "We couldn't handle it. It would have taken hundreds of people just to sort things out and address envelopes."

In late 1965, serious attention was given for the first time to establishing EDP as a major political tool. The ambitious idea was to put the name of every voter (and a bit of vital information about him) on a punch card.

But who were the voters? Arkansas had always been a poll-tax state, in which voters didn't register. Precinct boundaries were largely meaningless. "People voted wherever they felt like voting," says Burton. The problem was partly overcome in 1964 when an amendment to the state constitution was adopted establishing voter registration. The primary in 1966 was the first election in which voter registration was required.

It was on April 1, 1966, that EDP offices were opened in the Tower Building. At first, the only equipment was two aging key-punch machines. In charge of the day-to-day operation was Charles Nichols, an experienced computer programmer. His computer, the IBM 1401, arrived on July 1.

But before the computer could be used, volunteers had to be recruited to canvass the voting households. And, before volunteers could be sent into the streets, names and street addresses had to be obtained.

With no way to get data from official sources, the Rockefeller organization hired a company that specializes in tabulating mailing lists from telephone books. The company went through every telephone book in Arkansas and transferred names and street addresses to IBM punch cards, one card for every household with a telephone number.

These names, coming out of the telephone books, were in alphabetical order according to the boundaries arbitrarily set by the telephone company. Rockefeller workers had to sort the cards into precincts, by street and by house number. It was an immensely complicated job that wasn't helped by the fact that most of the precinct boundaries had been newly drawn. A further complication: Gaps in street numbers indicated that a surprisingly high number of Arkansas households didn't have telephones.

At this point, the information on the punch cards was rudimentary—a name, an address, a telephone number. More information—a great deal more—was required if the EDP system was to have political relevance. Information such as: how many people in the household; how many eligible to vote; how many registered to vote; political inclinations; occupations; ages; willingness to work for Rockefeller. All this information had to be solicited and then transferred to the IBM cards.

Volunteers were recruited and sent out into the precincts to collect the data. Some problems quickly surfaced: In what the Rockefeller people call "low-income Caucasian" districts, the volunteers weren't welcome. These, of course, are the historic segregationist areas in Arkansas where strangers—especially Rockefeller-Republican strangers—are suspect. In parts of rural Arkansas, the organization couldn't find many volunteers, so efforts to collect data there had to be abandoned.

Because of these and other problems, the organization decided to concentrate the campaign in Arkansas's thirty most populous areas, especially Pulaski County (Little Rock). And, in time, it became obvious that door-to-door canvassing was more work than the volunteers could handle. Teams of telephone volunteers, many of them college students, took up the slack. In Pulaski County, nine phones were in constant use for more than three months. By the time the job was finished, 90 percent of the homes in Pulaski County had been surveyed and all the necessary information transcribed on the IBM cards. Rockefeller, hardly as a matter of coincidence, carried Pulaski County by a 2-to-1 margin.

The information collected by the volunteers streamed into the "quiet room" in the Tower Building where twelve paid workers coded the information taken by the volunteers and passed it along to the key punchers. The key punchers —paid professionals too—put the coded information on the IBM cards. The "quiet room" processed as many as 16,000 cards every working day.

And, as the cards were being processed, the new computer was put to work. The first project was to isolate the people who showed an interest in Rockefeller but who were not registered to vote.* With a computer, isolating that kind of people—or, for that matter, any special category taken into account on the punch cards—is an easy job: You just run the cards through the computer, and out spill the names you're looking for.

---

* In many southern states, there have been literally hundreds of thousands of literate, hard-working people who have never bothered to vote. That's because so many of these states have been one-party Democratic, and it has been Democratic policy to keep the vote down, especially in primary elections.

Each person who seemed interested in Rockefeller was approached three times. First, the computer sent him a letter from Marion Burton, who was listed as "registration chairman." A follow-up letter was mailed through the computer from Rockefeller himself. Finally, volunteers telephoned these unregistered voters and made a personal pitch. The results speak for themselves: Registration jumped 60,000 from primary time in July to general-election time in November.

Computers can do all kinds of jobs, and writing letters is one of them. Mr. Rockefeller's IBM 1401 is equipped with a high-speed printer that can type out 600 *lines* a minute, equivalent to the output of 347 experienced typists. The IBM 360, to which Rockefeller is graduating, can type out 1,100 lines a minute, or the output of 636 typists. The finished product, coming out of either computer, looks exactly like a neatly typed letter from the machine of a good stenographer.

Following the registration deadline, the computer went to work processing literature for the direct-mail campaign. By the end of the campaign, the computer had helped to distribute more than 1,000,000 individual items—about two pieces for each person who voted. Much of the Rockefeller direct mail was pamphlets and brochures; the computer addressed the labels for these items.

Other campaign tools were used in the Rockefeller campaign. Television and radio, for example. And, of course, the candidate traveled around the state speaking and being seen and heard. But, the Rockefeller strategists insist, it was direct mail that won the election.

"We couldn't have won without it,"* says Marion Bur-

---

* Rockefeller defeated Johnson by 49,000 votes. His victory also carried into office a Republican lieutenant governor—Maurice "Footsie"

ton. "What we accomplished is pointed out by the fact that Jim Johnson [the Democratic candidate] got out his vote. But we cranked out *more* votes. The problem is apathy; people in Arkansas don't vote in big numbers. We get a total of 500,000 votes when we should get 900,000. So somebody isn't reaching the average guy in the average household. These people aren't interested because they don't think they're a part of it. They can turn off their television and they don't have to read newspaper ads. But when they get a personal letter from Winthrop Rockefeller, they react.

Two points. One, the candidate was a Rockefeller, which meant a "personal" letter had extraordinary interest to most people. Second, the average guy in that average household wasn't really getting a "personal" letter from a Rockefeller. He got a letter pushed through a computer, probably the most impersonal machine yet devised by man. Marion Burton doesn't think there's anything sinister about it. "What's the difference," he asks, "between me sitting down and signing letters or me authorizing a computer run-off of the same letters?"

For Burton, there is no difference. For the voter who

Britt, a one-armed winner of the Medal of Honor and one of Arkansas's great football heroes. But there were only three Republicans in the state legislature in 1967, and never-say-die Democrats wrote their own lyrics to the song "This Ole House":

> Ain't gonna bow to Rockefeller,
> Ain't gonna join the GOP,
> Ain't gonna pass his legislation,
> Gonna act constructively;
> Ain't gonna build his second party,
> Ain't gonna tamper with the law,
> Ain't gonna quit without a battle,
> Gonna save old Arkansas.

Democratic obstructionism seemed to be taking its toll on Rockefeller. In late 1967 the governor was putting on weight and showing signs of nervousness.

thinks someone finally cares about *him,* there may be a significant difference.*

Because governors in Arkansas are elected every two years, campaigning hardly ever stops. Late in 1967 Rockefeller's EDP machinery was at work as usual preparing for the 1968 elections. By then, the operation in Room 440 was smooth and professional. The files, once so chaotic, were neatly kept and bulging with information—the most complete political storehouse maintained anywhere in Arkansas. There were almost 200,000 IBM cards in the "survey file"; these are the cards that were punched out as a result of the door-to-door and telephone canvassing in 1966. More canvassing was under way in 1967 to expand and update the files. There are 65,000 more cards in the "special interest" file; it includes the names of members of various trade and professional groups, lawyers, real-estate men, doctors, and many, many more. Thanks to these files, Mr. Rockefeller can mail—almost overnight—special appeals to people with special interests.†

Then, there are an additional 50,000 cards in the "master file"; it includes names, addresses, and pertinent information about members of the Republican county committees, women Republicans, Young Republicans, even Democrats who dare not (in Arkansas) publicly acknowledge their Re-

---

* It is unpleasant to take my colleagues in the press to task once again. But, in the 1966 elections in Arkansas, no in-state paper saw fit to write a meaningful story about Rockefeller's use of a computer. Only one newspaperman visited the computer offices in the Tower Building, and he was from Tennessee. He wrote a frothy feature.

† This sort of thing is becoming widespread. Some colleges and universities now are putting the names of their alumni into similar files. Thus, an alumnus with a special interest in, say, the fine arts will be mailed a computer-printed letter, signed electronically by the president, detailing what the college is up to in the area of the fine arts. The possibilities for fund raising are obvious.

publican inclinations. It is a file, in fact, of all those people who have a close and abiding interest in GOP affairs.

Because IBM cards are bulky and because it takes time to move them through a computer, all these data are being switched from the cards to discs. The discs look very much like phonograph records, and the information is actually taken off them in the computer by a phonographlike needle. The standard IBM card such as the Rockefeller people use has space for only eighty entries; this obviously limits the amount of information that can be collated without making two cards for each subject. There is no such limitation with discs; any amount of information can be entered (more than 2,000,000 entries to every disc), and there's no storage problem. In EDP, the progression in sophistication is from IBM cards to tape to discs. Discs are far and away the most sophisticated, and expensive, way to store and to retrieve data. Anyone who has ever heard the eerie whirring of discs begins to get some idea of the incredible speed and efficiency of this system. Rockefeller will be using his discs in the 1968 election.

The Rockefeller people have every reason to be pleased with their EDP accomplishments. They will probably be the first organization in the nation to establish an EDP file for every voter in as large a political unit as an entire state. But Arkansas, after all, is not a very populous state. And Rockefeller has been using that IBM 1401 computer to perform nothing more than clerical functions.

I attended in September of 1967 a private, day-long meeting of politicians and representatives of one of the largest computer manufacturers in which the possible contributions of EDP to politics were discussed in considerable detail. Perhaps the most striking note to come out of that meeting was the utter surprise of the computer people that so little was actually being done in the political area.

"I had thought," said one of the industry representatives, "that the two national committees had been using computers for years." Not so, said one of the politicians: "When it comes to sticking with the status quo, never underestimate either the Republican or Democratic leadership at the national level."

We have already noted that the Democratic National Committee maintains an IBM 1401 in its Washington headquarters, and in late 1967 was preparing to move up to an IBM 360. True enough. But, as far as I can learn from inordinately closemouthed workers at the national committee, very little use has been made of the computer. First of all, it's used to process the committee's payroll, a simple enough procedure. Second, it's used to solicit funds and to maintain the fund-raising files. Once again, this is a rudimentary kind of clerical function. Finally, it is sometimes used to solicit funds for individual members of Congress who supply the national committee with data the computer can easily handle. And this is about all that the big computer and the people hired to work with it do. There must be, I suspect, considerable idle time. "It's ridiculous," says a highly placed Democrat who has observed the operation. "It's a waste of money."

The Republican National Committee has no computer, and doesn't plan to get one. In a way, the thinking at the two national committees is amusing. The Democrats keep a computer at the federal level in Washington; the Republicans want each state to get its own computer. A wonderfully petty example of the two historic philosophies at work.

The Republican National Committee, however, does contract with a computer service bureau to perform a number of clerical functions. Most of this work involves fund-raising activities. This same service bureau is used by the

Republican Congressional Campaign Committee and is available to individual Republican members of Congress.*

Even though it doesn't have a computer, the Republican National Committee has been a pacesetter in encouraging various party units to establish their own EDP systems. Much of this evangelical work has been performed by a young computer programmer from California, Edward J. Nichols, who was employed in 1967 as the national committee's data-processing consultant. Nichols, in fact, has written the only practical guide to EDP and its political ramifications I have ever seen.

Nichols's *Electronic Data Processing and Politics* stresses once again the clerical functions of EDP. He points out how a master file of names and addresses can be collected and how special mailings, especially for fund raising, can be made with such data. He also notes how EDP can be used in registration campaigns and in precinct canvassing. All this, of course, is the sort of thing that the Winthrop Rockefeller organization has been doing.

Nichols, however, does give some interesting twists. He writes:

> As the master file becomes more complete, mailings can become more sophisticated. For example, a prominent banker may be asked to write a letter to other bankers, a doctor to other doctors, and a farmer to other farmers. All these letters, and others, can be fed into and stored in the memory of the computer. The computer will then select all those people with the specified occupations, and write a personal letter to each. A space will be provided for the sender's name to be written

---

* The Republican National Committee also maintains an information retrieval system in which newspaper clippings and other relevant material are coded as to subject and category. "If a copy of a clipping is required," says a GOP manual, "the . . . system can supply one in a matter of seconds." Technically, however, this Recordak system is not EDP.

in ink, or a signature machine can sign the letters. The computer type will be indistinguishable from typewriter type. The pages are cut so that it is impossible to recognize it as computer output.

He gives other illuminating examples:

A new technique of public opinion sampling is to keypunch a card for each letter that is received by the candidate or incumbent. This card would contain information from the letter such as the sender's name, address, nickname if available, occupation, age and sex if available. This punched card could be coded as to the issue content of the letter (e.g., attitude on 14[b], or the War on Poverty). As letters come in, a simple open-ended public survey can be taken. With enough information, it would be possible to identify trends by groups or within areas of the district. With this information, the computer could print a personal letter thanking the writer for his specific remarks, and explaining the candidate's or incumbent's position. The computer could address him by name or nickname in the body of the letter.

For an incumbent, the names and addresses of visitors to the office can be put on punched cards. These cards could be coded to describe the nature of the visit, and subjects discussed. Once a year, Christmas for example, letters can be sent to these people. The letter or greeting would specifically recall items of interest.

Nichols's guide moves on to discuss another basic task EDP can perform in politics—one that Nichols calls demographic/political analysis:

A voter profile of a state or subdivision can be a very important item. This profile would describe each precinct or census tract division regarding past voting record, past and present registration, demographic data such as number of voting age residents, mobility, ethnic distribution, income, and other pertinent information. This profile could show voter turnout and loyalty. Correlations, such as registration and vote for Congress, can be produced.

Precisely. We have seen that the Romney organization already is doing some of this kind of computer-related work. But much of the thrust of the Romney effort, as we have noted, is to isolate the "ticket-splitter."

Others, too, are turning to this kind of analysis. Among them are two familiar names—Bill Roberts and Stu Spencer of Spencer-Roberts & Associates (Chapter Two). Spencer and Roberts have purchased a minority interest in Datamatics, Inc., whose offices are down the corridor from their own. Datamatics' president is Vincent P. Barabba, who was just thirty-one when he incorporated his firm in 1967. Barabba is his own best salesman. Here, in his own words, is his justification for computer-developed "social-area analysis":

Let us begin with one hard and tough assumption. That is, that present factual data concerning election districts are not adequate. For example, the U.S. Chamber of Commerce and other civic minded agencies provide what I will call aggregate data on certain Congressional districts. Considering what these organizations have to work with, they are probably doing the best job possible. However, what was adequate yesterday does not win elections today. Let me use one Congressional district to illustrate my point [the Twenty-second district in Los Angeles]. . . . If you had selected this district as a target area, how useful would this information [provided by the Brewster Map Company of Los Angeles and the United States Chamber of Commerce] be? In looking at the area-wide statistics you see that Barry Goldwater, in 1964, drew 46 percent of the vote, that Senator Murphy outdistanced Pierre Salinger two to one, that a fairly conservative Republican nominee lost to a very liberal Democratic incumbent by one percentage point. . . .

With these factors in mind you get a fairly good overview of voting habits in the district. When you look at the economic conditions you see that the area ranks significantly higher as far as income, level of education, value of home and type of work than the median for the city of Los Angeles. . . .

When you take a closer look at the district you soon find that it is really made out of 88 separate neighborhoods. What are the neighborhoods that make up this district? We use the U.S. Bureau of the Census definition of a neighborhood which is called a "census tract." A census tract is basically a geographic area which encompasses approximately 4,000 homogenous residents. . . .

If you take a close look at this entire district, you find out that there is great variance within it. You have, for one example, one census tract (1151) which has an average median income of $12,000, a level of education on the average of about the second year of college. . . .

You have another census tract (3203), which happens to be the southern portion of the city of San Fernando with about 70 percent of the population having Spanish surnames and an income level which makes them eligible for poverty funds—there are many people below a $3,000 annual income. Also, of all the people with Spanish surnames who live in the Congressional district, nearly three-quarters of them live in this census tract. . . . If you are going to communicate a message, you want to make sure that you put the message where it is going to be effective. For example, if you have a message that is of concern to Spanish speaking people which you do not want to *emphasize* throughout the whole district, you should pinpoint it where it is going to do you the most good. And this is the point that we want to make, that you have to find out where these *specific* areas are before you attempt to communicate with them.

Barabba goes on to note that no single map or analysis is complete enough to furnish all the data a campaign manager needs. The complete data are available, he says, but fragmented in a bewildering array of maps, summaries, and analyses. And so, says Barabba, "you are left in the Ancient Mariner's famous plight of 'water, water everywhere, nor any drop to drink.' Clearly, something better is needed." Just as clearly, of course, Barabba and his firm are ready and willing to supply that something better.

An old-school politician, at this point, might cry "Nonsense!" Such a politician thinks he knows his district; he lives in it, works in it, campaigns in it; he knows thousands of its voters. Barabba concedes that some politicians have a "feel for the area." After all, he says—in another of his allusions—"in the land of the blind the one-eyed man is king. But how many one-eyed men would refuse a second eye?"

The second eye is supplied by two Datamatics' systems—Social-Area Analysis and Precinct Index Priority System (PIPS).

Barabba has refined his Social-Area Analysis system so that it concentrates on three social variables—economic status, familization, and ethnic status.

Barabba's explanation for using "economic status" rather than the more familiar index—"income"—is interesting. "Income, we feel, is not a good designator of the ability to communicate to someone. You find situations where a teamster is making significantly more money than a college professor. In the state of Wyoming . . . you have trainmen in the Brotherhood of Railroad Workers who are making in excess of $12,000 a year." Thus, Barabba's index of "economic status" takes into account education and occupation.

The familization index is based on fertility ratio (the number of children under five in relation to women fourteen to forty-five), women who are not in the labor force (which is to say, housewives), and the owner-renter ratio (simply, the proportion of owner-occupied homes). A high score of familization, Barabba says, would be a neighborhood "in which most of the families have several children and they live in a single family owner-occupied dwelling unit and the wives generally are at home. This would perhaps be the *Ladies' Home Journal's* version of the ideal American way of life."

The third variable—ethnic status—is obvious enough. Race and nativity are the two principal components.

The Barabba method of graphically illustrating the information is wonderfully complicated. And imaginative.

Two of the variables—economic status and familization —are indexed. Each index is broken into four quadrants. For economic status, the figure "1" is low, "2" next to lowest, "3" next to highest, and "4" the highest. Familization gets letters. Thus, "D" is low, "A" high, and "B" and "C" are in between. "When we deal with economics, we deal with numbers," Barabba emphasizes—he too moves very slowly through his explanation—"and when we deal with familization we deal with letters. It is most important that you remember this distinction. And for those of you who remember the four-point system in college where $A = 4$, $B = 3$, $C = 2$, and $D = 1$, it might help you remember the order from high to low.

"I want to make it clear," Barabba continues, "that '4' in economics does not necessarily mean that the census tract will also be an 'A' which is high in familization. It could well be a 'B' or a 'C' or a 'D' in familization. You could have a '4B' district as well as a '4A' district. . . ."

So what do you have? Well, says Barabba, you have a workable description of each neighborhood. A "4A" district, he says, "would be an area in which there are very few people who have less than an eighth-grade education. It is an area in which of the labor force very few are classified as laborers, operatives, or craftsmen. As far as the familization rating, it is an area in which there are quite a few children. Most of the people live in single family owner-occupied dwelling units, and very few of the women are in the labor force. A '4B' district is the same as a '4A' district as far as economic characteristics are concerned. However, when it comes to the family, there is a possibility that they are either (1) living in multiple dwelling units or (2) have very few children in relation to families, or (3) the wife is in the labor force.

"The point we are making is that to communicate a message to a '4A' tract is significantly different from communicating a message to a '4B' tract. . . ."

But back to the graphics of it all. Barabba makes charts to illustrate his Social-Area Analysis. In these charts, he takes a deep, deep red to designate the lowest economic score. "It goes to a lighter red as the economic status increases until it comes into yellow. The same situation exists for familization; only, in this case we use blue, and again the lowest is the darkest, dullest color, and as it gets lighter and brighter you end up with the highest scores."

What happens when you combine the two charts? A coup for Barabba—the whole color spectrum! "We have used primary colors," he says, "and have now evolved a system which ranges over the entire color spectrum. This may be a cute trick as far as art students are concerned, but I think it has far greater implications. What you see is the fact that if you take a deep-blue color, which is low in familization, and a deep-red color, which is low economics, you end up with a purple. If you take a deep blue, for low familization, and a yellow, which is high economics, you come up with a green. Here we have two distinct colors and we do in fact have two distinct socioeconomic areas. These are basically different areas as they are different colors. We thus have the capability of not only coloring but also designating areas in 16 different ways."

By now, a skeptic might find his attitudes hardening. But Barabba has *used* this system in actual situations. The example he points to is his Social-Area Analysis of the city of Spokane, Washington. "Here," he says, "we have 49 census tracts, groupings of 4,000 to 5,000 people." The map is a gaudy collection of colored squares and rectangles. "Notice there is only one pure yellow district. That's census tract Number 42. Another thing that you might notice is that census tract Number 42 protrudes out of the normal city boundary lines. The reason that it protrudes is that it is a recently annexed area to the city of Spokane. And this is the new area of Spokane, the split-level homes, the children who have gone away to college and have come back, own their own homes, and have managerial-type positions, whose wives are not working and who have a lot of children running around the neighborhood."

Tracts 34, 35, 37, 38, and 39, in the southern part of the city, have the same economic standards—fairly good levels of education, fairly good jobs—but they are colored green. "These," say Barabba, "could very well be the parents of the people who live in Tract 42. They look upon such things as their schools and their taxes differently from their children."

Tract 6, in the eastern part of the city, is also colored green. "In this case it is a relatively new area, but here you have the distinction between single-family dwelling units and apartment houses, and the distinction between women *not* in the labor force and women *in* the labor force.

"Now we get down to real practical politics. If, for example, you believe in your candidate knocking on doors, then clearly you would go to Tract 42 during the day, preferably not during the children's napping hours, and Tract 6 during the evening because you are not going to find anybody home during the day. Tracts 34, 35, 37, 38, and 39 you do not want to hit when Lawrence Welk is on television. This is a very practical use of the device. You can go further, of course."

The third variable—ethnic status—is not a part of the

multicolored maps. Barabba seems to indicate that this over-
sight should be corrected by making a plastic overlay. It
seems reasonable.

So much for Social-Area Analysis, but it is only one-half
of the program Datamatics is willing to lay out for a candidate. The other half is the Precinct Index Priority System
(PIPS). "If Social-Area Analysis describes the kind of people
with whom you are dealing," says Barabba, "the Precinct
Index Priority System tells you how badly you need to deal
with them."

With PIPS, we are back on somewhat firmer ground.
The system is very much like the Romney organization's
method of isolating those voting districts in which chances
are high of winning a favorable outcome. "PIPS," says
Barabba, "is a device which functions to ensure that the effort
and funds of the campaign are channeled into areas of greatest potential return."

In an actual example of PIPS in action cited by Barabba,
data was collected about the candidate's primary vote; the
results of a vote on a constitutional amendment; the primary
vote of a candidate who had endorsed the client candidate;
and registration figures.

"Once obtained, the data is weighed, correlated, and introduced into a computer resulting in a rank ordering of
every census tract in the district on the basis of its potential
vote yield," says Barabba.

With PIPS, the candidate or the campaign manager can
assign volunteers scientifically, even to the point of noting
that young people should be used for hilly districts. The
computer can print-out letters to each volunteer, giving him
his assignment, the address of the place where he is to report, and the time when he is to complete his work. Once

again, the computer can handle direct mail, and decide what areas should get the mail.

Ideally, Barabba suggests, the client candidate should use both Social-Area Analysis and PIPS. For, with both systems, as Barabba suggests, Datamatics can show where the voters are and what they look like.

It is my own opinion that Datamatics tends to complicate unnecessarily what is essentially a rather simple EDP assignment, especially in the way it handles Social-Area Analysis. But can anyone really doubt Barabba's conclusion? "The candidate who does not avail himself of modern campaign techniques may be as unfortunate as the physician who shuns the latest diagnostic instruments or the businessman who disregards new methods of merchandising. It is a truism that in an era of innovation he who does not move forward is left behind." It is, for a fact.

We have now discussed two stages of development in the uses of EDP as a political tool. The first stage, for lack of a better phrase, might be called "list keeping." It's the sort of thing Winthrop Rockefeller is doing in the areas of registration, fund raising, and direct mail. The second stage is demographic/political analysis. It's the sort of thing Vincent Barabba is developing.

Once again, the Republicans are leaders in both areas.* Nichols, in his *Electronic Data Processing and Politics,* lists

---

* A word should be said here about the AFL-CIO's Committee on Political Education (COPE), which has been a quasi-official arm of the Democratic Party and which has turned in recent years to EDP. COPE uses EDP to maintain its files of union membership; these files, in turn, are used for various direct mailings and for some precinct work. One wonders, however, about the accuracy of such files. In the summer of 1967, COPE commissioned John F. Kraft, Inc., to poll union members. COPE was staggered to discover that almost 50 percent of all union members were living in the suburbs and that these suburban unionists accounted for 75 percent of all union members under the age of forty.

twenty-five Republican state committees that are using, or are about to begin using, EDP. Some of this state-level activity is already quite sophisticated. In California, for example, the state committee has compiled a demographic/political analysis of all the state Senate and Assembly districts. This data goes all the way back to 1958. In Louisiana, the Republican state committee processed some 500,000 IBM cards in 1964 with the help of 20,000 volunteers. The Republican State Finance Committee in Minnesota began using EDP in 1956. The committee at one time had its own computer.

The Republicans are also active at the county level. Orange County in southern California—one of the most conservative counties in the nation—is perhaps the leader. The GOP county committee has a special nine-man subcommittee working with EDP. Every registered voter is on tape, and the list is updated monthly. Precinct walking sheets are printed-out by computer and made available to every precinct captain, area chairman, division chairman, and Assembly district chairman.

But none of this really challenges a systems analyst or a computer programmer, for all of it is essentially a mechanical function. None of it really requires decision-making or even the building of a computer model. It is into these areas we now plunge, with some trepidation.

Ultimately, we shall discuss what is probably the most promising use for a computer in politics—simulation—but

---

The Kraft poll also showed that this new breed of unionist was hardly concerned at all with traditional union causes—right to work, for example, or minimum wage. They were interested in purely local issues—property taxes, sewer lines, schools. COPE, as a result, is switching its pitch from the cities to the suburbs. The only surprise is that it should have taken COPE so long to see the light.

first, we will take a brief look at some other possibilities:

1. Using a computer to place advertising. The big advertising agencies, such as Young & Rubicam, have been developing computer models of the entire national media. The data show the area covered by every radio and television station, the kind of audience that listens to each station —its age, median income, even its tastes. There are comparable data for newspapers and magazines. As far as I know, no candidate or party organization has ever tried to use a computer to place advertising—even though computers are already programmed to do just that. The benefits are obvious. Instead of guessing about the impact of television versus newspapers, the candidate could, presumably, make decisions with scientific rationale. The entire campaign budget for advertising could be prepared on the basis of the computer's reckoning. And the computer could even prepare the budget, mail the letters, and schedule the campaign.

2. Using a computer to schedule the events of an entire political campaign. Sometimes called the critical-path method (CPM), this already has been done in a number of special political campaigns. Old hands at the critical-path method are William H. Wilcox, executive director of the Greater Philadelphia Movement (a prestigious supercivic agency that has been responsible for much of that city's municipal renaissance), and James J. O'Brien, an engineer and CPM expert with Philadelphia's Meridian Engineering, Inc. Together, these two men have designed CPM systems that have been successfully used in Philadelphia to pass a referendum for a limited constitutional convention, eight amendments to the constitution, a school-charter amendment, and a stadium-bond issue. Wilcox and O'Brien have written:

> Today, volunteer citizen campaigns for and against referenda issues sometimes fall hopelessly behind schedule.

The reasons are: 1. too ambitious a program, 2. inadequate planning, and 3. too little manpower. . . . We have attempted to adapt to referenda campaigns a modern planning and management technique known as the critical-path method. This technique was first developed in the years 1956 to 1958 by a group of researchers at the E. I. du Pont de Nemours Co. . . .

The basis of the CPM technique is the arrow diagram, which starts at the beginning and is constructed independent of the desired goals. For instance, if we are going to purchase a car, there are three things we must do. First, we must decide what car we are going to purchase. Secondly, we negotiate for the new car, and, finally, we actually purchase the car. In arrow diagrams, these steps are represented in the following fashion.

Select new car model	Negotiate	Purchase new car
———→	———→	———→

These arrows represent logical sequences and say that we cannot start on the activity represented by the arrow until the preceding arrow has been completed.

Wilcox and O'Brien believe that they have been the first to apply CPM techniques to a civic program. They add: "Now that the application of network scheduling to election campaigns has been discovered, we predict early use of the method on a rather sophisticated plane for both issues and candidates at local, state, and national levels of government."

For the rather rudimentary requirements of a local campaign, a critical-path system can be developed (as it has been in Philadelphia) without the use of a computer. For anything more sophisticated, Wilcox and O'Brien agree a computer would be needed. Even without a computer, a CPM diagram can be complicated enough. Here is how one of those diagrams used in Philadelphia looks:

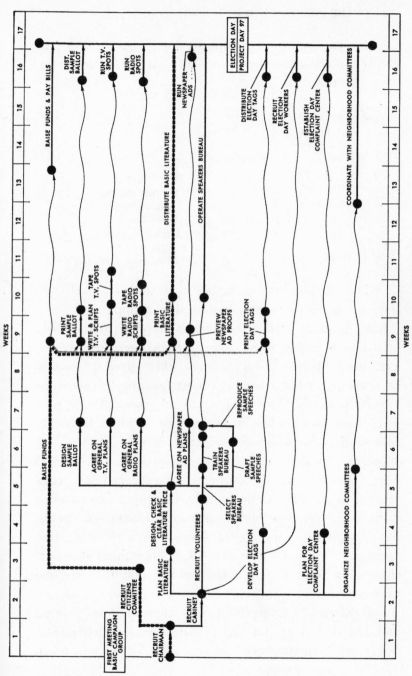

WEEKS

TIME SCALED CPM FOR REFERENDUM VOTE

GREATER PHILADELPHIA MOVEMENT

Meridian Engineering, Inc.

It is easy enough to compile a "campaign checklist" by simply following the diagram. Such a list would look something like this:

Minimum working days before election to start	Days to complete	Activity
97	5	Recruit chairman
92	10	Recruit citizens' committee
82	35	Raise funds
66	20	Organize neighborhood committees
66	7	Plan basic literature

The list, of course, continues right on down to Election Day. It's an interesting, and promising, technique.

3. "Gaming" with a computer. Computers already have been taught to play chess. The Pentagon uses them to play war games. The same kind of thing could be done for a political campaign. Essentially, as in most "gaming," it would be a teaching device. The computer is programmed with campaign data. One student makes a move in which his candidate speaks out on, say, civil rights. The other student—the opponent—makes a countermove. The procedure is followed from the beginning of the campaign to the end. The computer, finally, indicates the winner. Computer experts often spend their idle time playing this sort of game, just as the rest of us play a round of golf. I know one such expert who has been "gaming" with the 1952 Eisenhower-Stevenson election for years. So far, he has found no way for Stevenson to win.

Computer "gaming" is hardly an important political tool, but at least it's fun, and perhaps even instructive. This new, scientific politics needs an occasional bit of comic relief.

"Gaming," additionally, is a useful introduction to simulation, and simulation (as we have already stated) may turn out to be the computer's most important contribution to American politics. Not only to American politics, as a matter of fact, but to American business, to American government. "This [simulation] is the A-bomb of the social sciences," Yale University's Dr. Harold Lasswell has written. "The breakthrough here is comparable to what happened at Stagg Field."

What is simulation?

A simulation is an imitation of real-life processes. The computer amasses millions of individual bits of data. It digests this data and then suggests—estimates—what will happen in real life if any of a hundred courses of action are followed.

The key words are *what if*. What if a political candidate took a hard line on Vietnam? What if rioting in the cities grew much worse and a candidate proposed excessively harsh action? A poll can only indicate perceptions at a given moment in time. It is, in other words, static. A simulation estimates the range of human behavior hypothetically in a make-believe situation, but it's all mathematical and scientific.

And it seems to work. The first—and to date the only—political simulator was built for John F. Kennedy's presidential campaign in 1960. Instigating that project were Columbia University's William McPhee, MIT's Ithiel de Sola Pool, and Yale's Robert P. Abelson. These three men outlined their thinking to Edward L. Greenfield, a New York businessman and occasional adviser to liberal Democrats. Greenfield, in turn, alerted the Democratic Advisory Council to the possibilities of simulation. Working politicians, including Paul Butler, chairman of the Democratic National Committee, agreed to go ahead with the project, a surprising decision in light of the usual reluctance by politicians to experiment, and especially to experiment with anything so baffling to the layman as a simulator.

Absolutely vital to the success of the project was the accumulation of an immense amount of pertinent data. Such data was available at the Elmo Roper Public Opinion Research Center at Williams College, Williamstown, Massachusetts, where all the old IBM cards used by the Roper organization and by such other pollsters as George Gallup repose.

The Roper Center "agreed to permit the use of polls in their archives on two conditions," Pool and Abelson have written. "First, all basic data tabulated . . . from their cards were to be made available to the Center so the Republican Party would have an equal opportunity to use such data if they wanted them. . . . Second, and demanded by both the Center and the social scientists engaged in the project, all results could be published for scientific purposes after the election. . . ."

The principals—the social scientists and Greenfield—then organized themselves as The Simulmatics Corp. to allay criticism that they, and their universities, were accepting financial aid from "politically motivated sources."

The first step was to identify in the Center's archives all the polls that had been taken to anticipate the 1952, 1954, 1956, and 1958 elections. Later, polls taken for the 1960 election were added. "We selected those polls which contained standard identification data on region, city size, sex, race, socio-economic status, party, and religion, the last being the item most often missing. Further, we restricted our attention to those polls which asked about a substantial number of pre-selected issues such as civil rights, foreign affairs, and social legislation. From 1952 to 1958 we found 50 usable surveys covering 85,000 respondents. Sixteen polls anticipating the 1960 elections were added to this number. The 66 surveys represented a total of well over 100,000 interviews."

The next step was to divide these 100,000 or more respondents into representative voter types. Arbitrarily, the simulator-builders chose 480 distinct types. One of these 480, for an example, was: Eastern, metropolitan, lower-income, white, Catholic, female Democrat. Another was: Border state, rural, upper-income, white, Protestant, male Independent.

For each of these 480 types, information was recorded dealing with past voting behavior, election turnout, and attitudes on some 50 preselected issues. Altogether, there were some *one million* individual bits of information.

It was, as Pool and Abelson note, an "arduous" job. They give one example of the complexity. One of their "issue clusters" was "domestic communism or, as we called it for shorthand, McCarthyism. Over the past decade many questions have been asked on this and related matters in many different polls. One survey might ask: 'Are you in favor of permitting a Communist to teach in the school system?' Another would ask: 'What do you think of Senator McCarthy?' . . . The problem was to determine which questions tapped essentially the same attitude, domestic anticommunism." Obviously, a certain amount of smart, common-sense intuition was required.

Perhaps the most important question put to the simulator was, roughly, this: What would happen on Election Day if the anti-Catholic criticism of Kennedy became significantly stronger?

"The simulation," Pool and Abelson say, "required

that the computer make 480 calculations [one for each voter type]. . . . During each of the 480 calculations, the computer put into the equations values for turnout record, 1958 vote intention, 1956 vote intention, and anti-Catholicism, derived from the data which had been assembled about that particular voter type. This gave a 1960 vote estimate for each voter type for the particular hypothetical campaign being investigated."

The simulation estimates were "predictions of what would happen *if* the religious issue dominated the campaign. We did not predict that this would happen. We were describing one out of a possible set of campaign situations. But by August, when we took our national survey, comparison of our simulation and the survey results showed that this situation was actually beginning to occur. And the closeness of our contingent prediction to the final November result suggests that, indeed, the religious issue was of prime importance."

The simulation report on the religious situation was delivered to Robert F. Kennedy, JFK's campaign manager, on August 25. The key section reported: "If the campaign becomes embittered he will lose a few more reluctant Protestant votes to Nixon, but will gain Catholic and minority group votes. Bitter anti-Catholicism in the campaign would bring about a reaction against prejudice and for Kennedy from Catholics and others who would resent overt prejudice. . . . On balance, he would not lose further from forthright and persistent attention to the religious issue, and could gain."

The hypothetical situation the simulation considered did become a real-life situation, and John Kennedy had to make a decision what to do about it: He chose to meet the

religious issue squarely, and most post-election analyses indicate he made the right decision. But how much weight did
he give to the report from the simulator-builders? Reply
Abelson and Pool: "Neither we, nor the users, nor even
John F. Kennedy if he were alive, could give a certain answer. . . . [But] our own contribution, if any, was to bolster
by evidence one set of alternatives."

On the other hand, Theodore C. Sorensen, who was
closer to Kennedy than most, says the simulator reports
"were no more valuable than the 'issue polls' that were fed
into their computers. They contained all the same faults;
they restated the obvious, reflected the bias of the original
pollsters, and were incapable of direct application."

Except as a historical footnote, Sorensen's criticism is
academic. A simulator was built and it did supply information that was read by the ten or fifteen men who actually
ran a presidential campaign. More importantly, the simulator seemed to be at least partly effective.

Writing in April of 1964, Abelson and Pool took pains
to note that the 1960 simulation was rudimentary. "By
now," they wrote, "we know many ways in which to improve such election simulations. If we by any chance repeat
such research in 1968, it will be done differently in many
respects."

One major difference would be the computer itself.
The 1960 simulation was worked with an IBM 704 computer—"large and fast in that day but inflexible and slow
by present standards." In 1960 the simulator-builders developed those 480 representative voter types only because
the computer was unable to shuffle the 130,000 IBM cards
with sufficient speed. "The development of modern computers has made this transformation of individuals into

summary groups an unnecessary simplification. Today we could store and retrieve that many or more individual interviews."

The Simulmatics Corp., now a commercial firm with a growing list of clients (including a number of federal agencies), was, in the fall of 1967, ready and willing to build a simulator for the 1968 presidential elections. But no one had asked for one. Because time was growing short (the candidate would surely want the simulator working for him well before the convention, and he'd especially want it if he were campaigning in primaries), it appeared no simulator would be built for 1968.*

The computer experts aren't despairing, however. One of them told me: "Political simulators will be built, nationally and even on big-state levels, because politicians one day will realize you can't operate without them."

Perhaps so, but it will take time. Most politicians are still skeptical about using computers to handle payrolls, much less to construct models to imitate hypothetical, make-believe situations.

I confess that I remain uneasily skeptical about simulators. More than that, I'm worried about the ethical and moral problems they pose. We shall return to that problem in the final chapter. But, first, we'll examine one last campaign—John Lindsay's in New York City; for that campaign, on the face of it, seems to argue against certain presumptions we have made.

---

* The Romney organization was experimenting with the idea of building its own simulator in 1967. But, as far as I can gather, the cost—sometimes estimated as high as $250,000—was being viewed as prohibitive.

7

A POLITICAL ANACHRONISM:
THE LINDSAY CAMPAIGN
IN NEW YORK CITY

ROBERT PRICE, THE ABRASIVE LAWYER who managed John V.
Lindsay's winning campaign for mayor of New York, never
takes professional polls, and thinks political ads on radio
and television are usually just a waste of good money. Be-
lievers in the new scientific politics might dismiss such a
man out of hand—except that Bob Price has never lost an
election.

Price first met Lindsay in 1951; he was with Lindsay
in 1958, the year Lindsay was first elected to Congress. And,
in 1960, 1962, and 1964, Price managed Lindsay's campaigns. It was in 1964, too, that Price was lent to Nelson
Rockefeller. Price managed Rockefeller's Oregon primary
campaign, and it was the only primary that Rockefeller won.
Then, in 1965, Price topped it all off by electing Lindsay
mayor of the nation's largest and most impossible city.

It is, in the words of the King of Siam, a puzzlement. How can a man be so successful and at the same time be so old-fashioned? For the purposes of the thesis of this book, the problem goes deeper: Do you really need the new scientific politics after all?

If one takes the positive—that a candidate does need the new techniques—two possibilities are paramount. One, Lindsay was elected *in spite of* old-fashioned techniques. Two, Price's techniques weren't really as old-fashioned as they at first appear.

We shall suggest that both possibilities are relevant— that Lindsay won thanks largely to luck (his name was Buckley, an Irishman) and that Price's methods were not entirely old-fashioned. We shall also suggest that Lindsay could have won by a much larger margin if he had used just some of the new techniques. We shall first describe the Lindsay campaign as Price ran it off; then we'll suggest how the new techniques could have been used to immense advantage.

I—How It Was

What Price did in New York in 1965 was to establish a foot-soldier political organization, *ad hoc*. It was in many ways different from those old party organizations that still chuff and wheeze with a semblance of life in New York today. More precisely, Price created this new organization by opening and staffing 122 neighborhood, storefront headquarters in every section of the city. Out of a campaign budget of some $2,500,000, the storefront operation cost almost $1,000,000.

Techniques aside, it was a rouser of a campaign. Old Clem Whitaker would have loved every bloody minute of it, although I suspect he, like myself, would have found grievous shortcomings. It was not only a great fight but, thanks consciously to Bill Buckley, and unconsciously to the likes of Abe Beame and Mario Procaccino, it was a great show.*

Politically, New York City is a very special place. It is hardly a city at all; rather, it's five different cities, each with a flavor all its own. Outsiders tend to confuse Manhattan with New York City. Manhattan is the New York *Times*'s city; it's Wall Street and Broadway and the Empire State Building. It's the Plaza and women walking poodles on Park Avenue. Barbara Carter, in her *The Road to City Hall: How John V. Lindsay Became Mayor,* makes an important point: "But dusty Brooklyn has the votes. Some 1.1 million were registered there in 1965, compared to 775,000 in Manhattan. And dreary Queens has the votes, some 200,000 more than Manhattan. For all its topless towers, Manhattan ranked only third, not much larger than the Bronx, and since has fallen to fourth place. . . . Brooklyn, the City of Churches, has more people than Los Angeles; Queens only slightly less than Philadelphia. . . . Manhattan is about the size of Detroit . . . and the Bronx can swallow up Boston and San Francisco together. Little-noticed Staten Island . . . is the equal of Virginia's proud Richmond."

New York is, in fact, just one helluva big place, so big that most people who have lived there all their lives never get to know more than a little corner of it.

For a politician trying to govern such an immensity, the question of communication becomes staggering. There are literally thousands of special-interest groups; observing

---

* Procaccino, running for city comptroller on the Beame ticket, has become something of a legend. He concluded one of his campaign speeches by saluting Frank O'Connor, another running mate, with these words: "He grows on you just like cancer."

picket lines at City Hall for just a day or two is evidence enough of that.

And the problems. Lord, the problems. Crime (an average of two murders a day); air pollution; racial tension; unemployment; traffic congestion; schools. If anywhere in the world there is an urban problem, you can find it in New York City as well.

For twelve long, desperate years, Robert F. Wagner tried to *cope*. In March of 1965, the mayor reported in a speech at Long Island University what he had done, and what might be done. "I wonder who, in all honesty, would say that these problems are susceptible of solution by any collection of simple formulas," he said. "It is clear that since the problems originated outside the borders of the cities, the city government cannot be expected to cope with them unaided." The solution, he suggested, must be a federal one.

But, at the same time, the mayor was defensive; a lot, he said, had been done under his leadership. Building construction was on the upsurge—to an estimated $693,400,000 for 1965. Retail sales in 1964 totaled $12.2 billion. The city's private payroll was $5.3 billion. The city's budget, he said, was second only to the federal government's. The money was being spent to solve problems. "Enough new housing," he said, "has been constructed in New York City within the past ten years to house the entire city of Baltimore." And yet, and yet . . . "It is still a fact, however, that one million New Yorkers live in substandard housing accommodations."

The mayor concluded on the upswing: "In general, I would say that we in New York City are on top of our problems, in the sense that we are actively coping with them. We are overcoming some of them."

In that same speech, the mayor said: "Of course the cities are overwhelmed with new problems. But solutions will be found. Progress will be made. I wouldn't be trying to stretch twelve years as mayor of New York into sixteen if I weren't full of hope that this would be so."

It was anticipated, then, that Wagner would seek a fourth term. After all, he was practically an institution himself. He was first elected mayor in 1953, supported by the Democratic organizations (Tammany is the Manhattan organization, and is no worse than the others). But Wagner was not a machine Democrat himself, not quite. His chief asset was his name; he was the son of a great liberal senator whose memory is still cherished today by hundreds of thousands of New Yorkers.

Wagner's opponents in 1953 were Harold Riegelman, the Republican, and Rudolph Halley, the candidate of the Liberal Party. The Liberal Party is a singular New York phenomenon (as we first observed in Chapter Five). It has been led for years by those two aging trade unionists David Dubinsky and Alex Rose. Its leadership is often tyrannical and inclined to wheeler-dealership. Its membership is often precisely the reverse—emotional, idealistic, impractical. Over the years, however, the party has been a factor in a number of close, important elections. It was, as we shall see, a factor in the 1965 election. In 1953, the combined Republican and Liberal vote actually added up to a higher total than Wagner's.

By 1957 Wagner had mended his fences to the point that this time he won the endorsement of the Liberal Party. As a result, he easily defeated another faceless Republican—Robert K. Christenberry.

There is, it should now be noted, another singular phenomenon in New York City—the reform Democrats whose trinity is Herbert Lehman, Eleanor Roosevelt, and Adlai Stevenson. The reformers fight each other and, in fits and starts, fight the various Democratic organizations who tend to fight each other too. It is, all in all, a wonderfully baroque situation for which the onlooker needs a new scorecard about once a week.

Late in his second term, Wagner was under a typical cross-pressure—suspect by the Democratic organizations, the reform Democrats, and his old friends the Liberal Party leadership as well. What to do? Wagner, if nothing else, is a subtle politician with an uncanny sense about the things that motivate people. He sensed everyone's dissatisfactions properly, and came out foursquare as a renascent reformer. As a result, he won back the confidence of the reform Democrats and the endorsement of the Liberal Party. He was reelected to a third term in 1961, defeating a better than usual Republican opponent, Louis J. Lefkowitz, by some 400,000 votes. A protest candidate, Lawrence E. Gerosa, running on the Citizens Party ticket (his own creation), managed to win 321,000 votes, however. Many of those votes came from working-class Democrats whose inclinations were, like Gerosa's, conservative. It was a portent.

Thus, early in 1965, Wagner—a three-time winner—was expected by everyone to be the Democratic candidate once again. And most people thought that once again he would be the choice of the Liberal Party. Most people thought, too, that the reform Democrats would vote for him, having nowhere else to go.

Astute Republicans realized that Wagner, for all this, was vulnerable. The accumulated disappointments of twelve years were catching up. Wagner was tired, and he looked tired—and so did his administration. But, after all, the registration in the city gives the Democrats almost a $3\frac{1}{2}$-to-1 edge. And there was that great tradition of Riegelman, Christenberry, Lefkowitz. The Republicans needed a big leaguer, not another Met.

Given such a situation, eyes naturally turned to John Lindsay. In 1964 he carried his congressional district—the so-called "silk-stocking" Seventeenth—by 91,274 votes at the same time President Johnson was carrying the district by 85,195 votes. Lindsay's victory percentage (71.5) was the greatest of any opposed Republican congressional candidate in the country. And it is worth noting that his Democratic opponent, Eleanor Clark French, was endorsed by the Liberal Party.

The Seventeenth District, however, is hardly New York City in microcosm. It runs, roughly, from Third Street in Greenwich Village all the way up to 110th Street and from the East River across town to Eighth Avenue. Within its boundaries are the United Nations, the Metropolitan Museum of Art, Rockefeller Center, Stuyvesant Town and Peter Cooper Village, and the garment center and Yorkville. The 1960 census reported that its median family income—$8,649 —was the fourth highest in the country and that the median number of school and college years for its adult population —12.6—was also fourth in the nation.

In his years in Congress, Lindsay nicely reflected his district's thinking. He was eminently respectable—liberal but not too liberal, hard-working but not a bore about it. He outraged traditional, more conservative Republicans by voting for the Democrats as often as he voted for his own party's positions. Especially aggravating were his votes in 1961 and 1963 to enlarge the House Rules Committee. The New York Young Republican Club (of which Lindsay was president in 1952) censured him for his antiparty attitude. He was a member of the Wednesday Club, a group of progressive Republican congressmen, and he was one of four floor managers in the House for the 1964 civil-rights act, but all in all his record as a legislator and as a leader was not overwhelming. He tended, most thought, to go his own route, alone.*

Lindsay, in fact, may have been the kind of politician Daniel J. Boorstin has written about in his *The Image or What Happened to the American Dream*. Writes Boorstin: "National politics (with the full paraphernalia of make-up, rehearsals, and kleig lights) has adopted the star system which dominates it more with every election. Yet anyone— or almost anyone—can be transformed into a star. . . . A star, then, must allow his personality to dominate his work; he is judged by his personality in place of his achievement."

John Lindsay does have a forceful and attractive personality. He is one of the most ruggedly handsome men ever to run for high office. He is a fine athlete and a good actor. He enjoys being the center of attention and he is willing to work very hard to place himself in that kind of situation. But he was not terribly enthusiastic about running for mayor.

"It's never good to lose," he kept telling those who urged him to take on Wagner. Lindsay and Price were impertinent enough to lay down a set of minimum requirements that would have to be met before they would consider running. First, they said, they needed guarantees that $1,-500,000 would be raised. Second, they wanted to be able to handpick their running mates. Third, they wanted to create an independent organization. Fourth, they wanted to open the campaign as early as March 1, 1965. Nelson Rockefeller passed the word that he and the state party could meet the first three conditions, but not the fourth. March 1 was far too early; the state legislature would still be in ses-

---

* Why was Lindsay a Republican in the first place? Asked precisely that question in 1963, Lindsay replied: "Well, it always sounds so trite. Heritage has a lot to do with it. My father was a Republican, though he didn't always vote for the Republican Party. He voted for Al Smith."

sion, and the governor didn't want young Lindsay attacking the Democrats at a time when he needed them to pass bills in Albany.

March 1 came and went, and Lindsay was out of it. Republicans met to consider the likes of John J. Gilhooley and Mario Biaggi, in the great losing tradition of Harold Riegelman and Robert K. Christenberry.

But was Lindsay ever really out of it? One wonders. The evidence suggests that Robert Price began thinking of running Lindsay for mayor as early as 1962. Not only thinking, but planning. Price is, to be sure, a native son, but the detailed knowledge of the city he displayed *immediately* after Lindsay announced his candidacy indicates preplanning. "The geographical knowledge of the city Price displayed could not have been put together that fast," says a man who worked at a high level in the campaign. "He knew the city intersection by intersection. He had reviewed the returns from all of the 5,000 election districts through the years, and he knew precisely where the key districts were."

Whatever the truth of it, the suspense—real or calculated—ended on May 13 with Lindsay's announcement that he was a candidate, personally delivered at stops in all of New York's five boroughs. "I enter this fight because conscience and duty compel me and because I believe that with proper leadership our city can once again be restored as the Empire City of the world." Let us, he seemed to be saying, get New York City moving again.

So there it was—Lindsay versus Wagner.

On June 9, Vice-President Humphrey told a New York audience that he had a feeling that Wagner in the days ahead would once again be mayor of New York. The very next day, Wagner called a press conference, presumably to announce he was a candidate for a fourth term. His opening remarks were hardly indicative of a change of heart. But then he got to the cruncher: "Simply put," he told a staggered roomful of reporters, "my decision is to end my service as mayor on January 1, 1966. I shall not seek or agree to reelection. . . . My decision, based on long and painstaking personal contemplation, and on consultation with my [two] sons, with other members of my family and with intimate friends, is final and irrevocable." Tears came to the old warrior's eyes, and when he was through the reporters gave him a heartfelt round of applause.

Within hours, the scramble began to fill the vacuum. Franklin D. Roosevelt, Jr., thought about it, and listened to people tell him he was the logical man to run. But he decided against it. Then Frank D. O'Connor, the popular district attorney of Queens, gave the idea some thought; but he decided he'd wait until the next year and run for governor. Ultimately, four Democrats entered the race, and a grab-bag collection they were: Paul R. Screvane, Wagner's president of City Council and the beneficiary of the mayor's good wishes; little Abraham D. Beame, the City Comptroller; Congressman William Fitts Ryan, the favorite of the far-out left; and City Councilman Paul O'Dwyer, who decided to run just for the hell of it.

Screvane was the odds makers' favorite. He had been a first-rate administrator and he had the mayor's support, wishy-washy as it sometimes appeared. Ryan and O'Dwyer were also-rans. That left Abe Beame, tarnished because he was the personal choice of Stanley Steingut, machine leader in Brooklyn; that calcified war-horse, Charley Buckley of the Bronx, and Harlem's Adam Clayton Powell.

Once again, however, party professionals showed just how little they really know about the way campaigns are run and won these days. The Screvane forces, supposedly the sharpest of the lot, misread the polls. With only a month to go, according to Peter Maas and Nick Thimmesch, the two able chroniclers of the Lindsay campaign, Oliver Quayle's polls showed Screvane with 51 percent of the vote and Beame with only 33. Screvane relaxed.

Beame, however, had two things going for him: He was Jewish in a city with a large and sometimes sophisticated Jewish population, and he had the most salable issue—that he was the one Democrat who had regularly challenged Wagner.

Primary Day was September 14, and little Abe Beame won it; he defeated Paul Screvane by 59,000 votes.

Finally, then, it was Lindsay versus Beame. And one other too—gadfly William F. Buckley, Jr., founder and resident guru at the *National Review*. He had declared his candidacy back in June, and everybody knew he was running only to deny victory to Lindsay. Buckley considered (and considers) Lindsay a renegade Republican whose blackest sin was his inability to find in his heart that Barry Goldwater was right for the Grand Old Party.

Perhaps, after all, Buckley had a point. Lindsay wasn't just everybody's kind of Republican and, anyway, he wasn't even planning to run as a Republican. The Lindsay ticket was a fusion ticket, including a Liberal (Timothy W. Costello) and a Democrat (Milton Mollen). Somehow, too, Buckley had got hold of a transcript of a session in which a committee of Liberals had screened Lindsay in a question-and-answer saliva test. Here are some of the relevant passages that add up to heresy for Buckley-minded conservatives:

QUESTION: Will you, if elected mayor of New York, use the office of mayor for the purpose of building up the Republican Party?

LINDSAY: No, under no circumstances. . . . As an individual who is a Republican, I would support a Republican candidate where he was deserving of it. I would not support a candidate of my party if he was not deserving of it. You know that I did not support the Republican candidate for President in 1964. If I felt it was necessary to give personal endorsement in my private capacity to the Republican candidate for office I would want to get as far away from City Hall as possible when I did it.

QUESTION: Are you for repeal of 14(b) [the right-to-work section] of the Taft-Hartley Act?

LINDSAY: I am for repeal. It is not good or right for labor within the free-enterprise system.

QUESTION: What do you think of co-operative housing in the framework of free enterprise?

LINDSAY: We must encourage the co-operative method in the economy. In fact, in the question of housing in which co-operatives are so vital, I have always felt that housing in a crowded city as New York should be regarded in the nature of a public utility. . . .

It was no real wonder, then, that the screening committee recommended fusion with Mr. Lindsay to the party's policy committee, that the policy committee approved the recommendation, and that the party members concurred in a party rally at the old Hotel Astor. Lindsay was their man, even though they had endorsed his opponent in his last congressional race.

Lindsay, the Republican-Liberal candidate, had a number of campaign alternatives. One, of course, he rejected out of hand—running openly as a Republican against the Democrats. Another possibility was running a strictly personality show-biz campaign. He could go heavy on television and radio, overcoming all with his rugged profile and glistening smile. Or he could use television as his prime medium to communicate his serious concerns to the electorate.

He, or rather Bob Price, rejected all those possibilities.

Price chose to run what he likes to call a "retail campaign." That means he chose to take his product—Lindsay—and march him through every neighborhood in New York, twice or three times if at all possible.

It was, as we have suggested, the kind of campaign Price had long considered. It was, in fact, the kind of campaign Price ran for Rockefeller in the 1964 Oregon primary. It set the pattern.*

Price first arrived in Oregon on April 6, 1964, the day after the Gallup poll reported that Rockefeller was the choice of only 6 percent of the nation's Republicans. He was hardly doing much better in Oregon; Henry Cabot Lodge was leading with 46 percent; Nixon was second at 17 percent; Goldwater third at 14 percent, and Rockefeller fourth and dead last at 13 percent. The election was May 15, which gave Price a little over a month to perform a miracle.

"When I first went out there [to Oregon]," says Price, "I figured the governor needed some exposure. I had always been impressed with clean storefront headquarters, starting when I worked in the Bronx when I was just seventeen or eighteen. So I decided riding out there in the airplane that we would go retail with the governor and open storefronts in each of the thirty-six counties in the state.

"Storefronts, you know, work even better in rural areas than they do in cities. When you open a store in a place like Bend or Fossil, you get some real attention. You open a store in Brooklyn and maybe no one will notice."

---

* It has been suggested that the storefront technique was an outgrowth of Lindsay's congressional campaigns. Not so. The Seventeenth District is geographically so small that the storefront—which in fact is a kind of campaign outpost—was of little value. The general idea of retail campaigning, however, *was* an outgrowth of district experience.

Price arranged to have letters written to 300,000 Republicans in Oregon, seeking support for Rockefeller. From the replies he chose his thirty-six county chairmen. Each time he chose a new chairman, he took out a big advertisement in the local papers, announcing the event. The ads also announced the location of the county's storefront headquarters.

"These storefronts drew people," says Price. "Our slogan was 'He Cared Enough to Come' and when he traveled around the state he came to these storefronts. We brought political activity to the overlooked parts of the state and in a primary it's Republicans from places like Klamath and Ontario who really turn out."

Rockefeller carried Oregon by 15,000 votes, and the storefronts were at least partly responsible. As Price says, "they [the storefronts] took us retail directly to the people who hadn't had the benefit of knowing they didn't like the governor."

It was two days short of a full year later that Lindsay announced he would run for mayor, with Bob Price guiding him along the way. And Price was ready. By the second week in June, the men he had recruited were meeting regularly in his office to hear precisely what they should be doing. Price's lectures were illuminated by huge maps that showed every street and house number in the city.

"I was assigned to ten Assembly districts in Brooklyn," says Robert M. Blum, "and for fully a month Price's knowledge of my area far outstripped my own. It was incredible. Somebody would suggest opening a storefront at, say, Bell Boulevard and 132nd Street. Price would think about it and then say, 'No good, that's two blocks away from the point of heaviest traffic. There's an empty store next to the movie theatre. Try that instead.' It was literally a tour de force. He must have put in 150 or more hours just walking and driving all over the city."

A sixteen-page "Manual for Organizing Campaign Headquarters in the City of New York" was written late one night, after a couple of martinis and a good rare steak, by Price's chief deputy, Constantine Sidamon-Eristoff (who later became Mayor Lindsay's commissioner of highways). The manual was mimeographed and distributed prior to June 1, still another indication that campaign planning had begun a lot earlier than the timing of Lindsay's announcement would indicate. The manual is an interesting document. Although written by Sidamon-Eristoff, it is a distillation of the Price method of running political campaigns. It is, as we shall suggest later, an anachronism in these days of mass-media campaigning. But it did work—to the extent that a functioning organization was created precisely along the lines recommended in the manual. It was no mean achievement. The manual reads:

> You are being asked to assume responsibility for the most important part of John Lindsay's campaign for mayor. Your job is to organize the foot troops—the local campaigners. You are going to be Neighborhood Campaign Managers for Lindsay. Each of you will be the campaign manager for one of 75 Assembly Districts in the City of New York. There you will open, man and run a Lindsay for Mayor headquarters through election day. Your neighborhood will be your whole life in the months to come.

The manual set a June 12 deadline—less than a month following Lindsay's declaration—for the opening of one key neighborhood headquarters in each borough. June 19 was the deadline for the opening of four more headquarters per borough. July 5 was the deadline for opening a headquarters in each of the city's 75 Assembly Districts.

"Once you select the A.D. in which you will work," says the manual, "go out there, walk its streets, learn its sub-neighborhoods, and immerse yourself in its life. Spend a day or two learning its problems. Live there as much as possible from now on—through November 2nd." As the manual indicates, the district campaign managers were largely carpet-baggers; most of them were from Manhattan, where they had known and worked for John Lindsay. These district managers reported to twelve or thirteen higher-level managers called "borough co-ordinators"; they too were mostly carpetbaggers. Lindsay's campaign was run by bright young men fanning out of the "silk-stocking" district into parts of the city some of them may never have glimpsed before in their lives. They survived under these adverse conditions because they had energy, devotion, and an esprit that survived the campaign.*

The 122 storefronts ultimately opened by the Lindsay organization achieved various levels of success. Each, however, had certain stated goals. First of all, every storefront was designed as a physical reminder that there really was a John Lindsay running for mayor and that he was running hard enough and caring enough to bring his campaign to that neighborhood. Those storefronts in Oregon served the same purpose.

But there was much more. The original idea was that every *non*-Republican voter would be personally contacted by volunteers working out of the storefronts. The Republicans, such as they were, were left to the regular Republican

---

* Lindsay's press secretary in late 1967 was Harry O'Donnell, an old Rockefeller hand. O'Donnell is one of the best political press secretaries anywhere, but the old storefront workers still consider him an outsider. A reporter seeking storefront information deals with storefront alumni, not O'Donnell.

organization. In the "Eristoff Manual," the Assembly District managers were told:

> Obtain and train 40 or 50 E.D. [Election District, or precinct] captains, one or more for each election district, and direct canvassing from prepared cards for the election. Cards will be distributed through borough co-ordinators as will an instruction manual. This will be your most important job. Our goal is to ring every doorbell in the City of New York. Incidentally, in assigning captains, if you are lucky enough to find any who have been E.D. captains for the Democrats, do not assign them to their old districts: this will save them much resentment and possible future trouble.

The cards supplied to the Assembly District managers —and then distributed to the precinct volunteers—were simple three-by-five index cards listing the name and address of every voter within the election district. It was up to the volunteer to sort the cards in consecutive order by street number, separating the odd side of the street from the even "so you won't waste time when you start canvassing."

The volunteers were instructed to make a personal visit to every one of the registered voters and conduct an interview to determine: Yes, he will vote for Lindsay; no, he is opposed to Lindsay, or maybe, he is in doubt. "Throw away the no cards," says the workers' manual. "Save the maybe cards for another visit during the month of October. Before you return in person, see that the maybe voter is supplied with Lindsay material—get him on a mailing list—answer his questions—find out what is causing him to hesitate. If after your second visit in October, he is still not a *definite* yes vote for Lindsay, throw away his card. Your yes cards are your Gold Nuggets—treasure them and put phone numbers on each card. You won't have time to look up phone numbers on election day."

The manual gives some helpful tips. Among them: "If you are in an apartment building . . . arrange your interviews so that you start at the top of the building and work your way down. You will find this is easier on your wind." Another: "If the building should have a doorman, smile and be friendly. . . . If the doorman will not let you in at all, then try another time when there's a different doorman on duty."

Thus, there is this point to be made: The Lindsay storefront operation was highly organized and precisely planned. It might even have been sophisticated because, in a point rarely noted, Price had hoped to use computers and data processing to back up his local organizations. A team of data-processing experts began work before Wagner withdrew from the race.

"What we had hoped to do," says Robert Blum, "was to give our storefront managers the special insights that a Stanley Steingut [Democratic chieftain in Brooklyn] would have. For example, Steingut and his people would know better than to go into an apartment house occupied 80 percent by civil servants and tell them how you're going to cut the budget. We wanted to avoid that kind of thing."

The computers actually did print-out information for every election district in the city. Data included the vote in the 1961 election (Wagner versus Lefkowitz and Gerosa) and the 1962 election (United States Senator Jacob K. Javits versus James B. Donovan). It also included the registration figures as of January 1, 1965, and went on to show income levels taken from 1960 census data. It listed the ethnic breakdown, number of people eligible to vote, and the number who actually did vote in the 1961 and 1962 elections.*

---

* The 1964 figures were not included. With Goldwater heading the GOP ticket, the figures were so lopsided for the Democrats as to be meaningless.

But the programming presumed Wagner would be the opponent. When Wagner withdrew, the presumption collapsed. And it wasn't until September 14 that Abe Beame emerged as the primary winner. The program was further delayed because many of the election districts had been reapportioned. As a result, the data wasn't available until the second week of October (it had been scheduled to be available in August). It was used, but not very successfully.

It is one thing, however, to read handbooks and manuals and examine data from computer print-outs. It's quite another to observe an actual storefront in operation. I spent three days in mid-October examining the operations of these storefronts, and the storefronts run by Ira Kellman, then a twenty-five-year-old Brooklyn lawyer, were typical.

On the day that Lindsay announced his candidacy, Kellman, a lifelong Democrat, fired off a telegram to Price. "What can I do?" it read. "When can I start?" A week later, the bright, aggressive Mr. Kellman went to work as the Lindsay coordinator in the Fifty-second Assembly District in the heart of Brooklyn, supervising the operations of two storefront headquarters.

The Fifty-second District is, of course, overwhelmingly Democratic. It's crescent-shaped: The northern section is heavily Negro; the central section is mixed; the lower section is heavily Jewish.

"People here think a Republican has horns and spits fire," Kellman told me. "That's why, as you've probably noted, the word 'Republican' doesn't appear anywhere in our headquarters." Voters were constantly reminded that Lindsay was running on three lines on the ballot—Republican, Liberal, and Independent Citizens, a special "party" formed just for the election, presumably to give a handful of voters who didn't want to vote on either the Republican or Liberal lines a place to go.

Like so many other managers, Kellman had his problems. He opened his first storefront in the southern (or Jewish) section of the district. The empty store—it had 6,000 square feet of space and hadn't been used for five years—was, in Kellman's words, "a mess." It took 200 man-hours of volunteer time to clean it up. In came the bunting, the desks, the chairs, the telephones. By then, says Kellman, the place looked attractive—so attractive that the owners found a regular tenant. Kellman and his volunteers had to move out.

This first store was below Church Avenue. The second store, into which Kellman and his volunteers moved in July, was above Church Avenue. Church Avenue is a dividing line; people who live below it stay below it; the people above it never go below it. It is typical of the structure of many New York neighborhoods. "This meant," says Kellman, "that we lost our original office workers and had to start all over to recruit new ones."

The other storefront, which became the *second* storefront, was at 630 Flatbush Avenue. It was an abandoned grocery story, a dusty freezer still lining one wall. Lindsay literature was piled high atop it.

"This [Flatbush Avenue] headquarters is important," Kellman told me. "People walk by out there"—he pointed out the window to the busy street—"and when they look in here they see their friends and neighbors. Some people, you know, think Lindsay is Rockefeller's relative or something. But when they look in here they don't see Nelson Rockefeller; they see people like Lucy Grossman, Joan Riegel, and Rabbi Sam Schrage."

Rabbi Schrage was especially helpful. He was one of the founders of the Maccabees, a group of Jews, many of them rabbis, who began riding night patrols in 1964 after the murder of a young woman in an elevator in the Crown Heights section. The Maccabees were generally credited in the area with cutting down the crime rate.

"When people see the rabbi here," Kellman observed, "they say to themselves, 'Well, Lindsay can't be all bad.' "

Kellman divided the Lindsay campaign in the Fifty-second Assembly District into two phases. The first phase, lasting from early June through Labor Day, involved getting Lindsay's rather unfamiliar name before the local community. "We made a lot of noise," Kellman said. "We had block parties with rock-and-roll bands; we put up posters and placards. We opened the two headquarters and plastered the windows with signs. And we collected our volunteers. It wasn't easy, I'll tell you. They just didn't fall in off the street. But we got them, about two hundred in all. We trained them in telephone and door-to-door canvassing; we developed some of our own telephone pitches. We got the cards for each of the 75,000 voters in this district, and we sorted them all by street, by building, and alphabetically. Then we looked them up in the reverse telephone book [which lists numbers by street address, rather than by name] and wrote their telephone numbers on the cards.

"We were ready to roll into the second phase by Labor Day. But we couldn't because the primary wasn't until September 26; we didn't know who the opponent was going to be. Then right after the primary we had the newspaper strike. Our candidate couldn't get moving because he couldn't talk about the issues when the Democrats were fighting their primary. And when that was over he couldn't start making real news because the papers were out."

For Kellman, the outcome of the Democratic primary was bad news because the winner, Abe Beame, was a Brooklyn Jew. Kellman wanted Screvane, a Queens Catholic, to win. "If Screvane were the candidate now," Kellman told me in mid-October, "we could get enough Jewish votes in this district so that Lindsay would actually win it. But as soon as Beame was nominated, we were in trouble."

Kellman reported that his workers were being told that the voters were going to vote Jewish and vote Democratic. The second phase of the campaign—the actual canvassing—began late in September, after the Democratic primary. Kellman's volunteers made a special appeal to Jewish voters, urging them to consider Lindsay on his merits—and to consider Beame on his demerits (support from the machines, connections with Wagner, narrow grasp of big problems).

Not every voter was canvassed in the Fifty-second District. But Kellman's volunteers did manage to visit or to telephone a very high proportion of the Democrats, Liberals, and independents. Their reception, reported Kellman, was generally good. "People here have been taken for granted for years," Kellman explained. "No one ever has rung my doorbell. The Democrats have never done it because they didn't have to. The only reason any of them work at all is because most of the [Democratic] clubhouses give a vacation in Florida to the captain who turns out the biggest vote."

Lindsay did not carry the Fifty-second District, but he came closer than some people thought he could. The vote: Beame, 18,758; Lindsay, 15,431; Buckley, 3,003.

Bob Blum, who was Kellman's boss, has given a lot of thought to the storefront operation and has evolved some theories of his own to explain their apparent success.

"They were efficient," Blum says, "because they were all singular. Each of them took on a flavor of its own, adapting to its own neighborhood. With an institutionalized organization, you couldn't have done that.

"The organized clubs [the Republican and Democratic

clubhouses] have a history. The people who belong work their way up through the chairs. They have their own built-in loyalties, and their relationships to all the various elected officials are open and committed. Can a club like that work with a candidate who has different points of view than the officials to whom they're committed? I don't think so. Once you become institutionalized, you lose flexibility.

"We could open one storefront in Cypress Hills, a conservative Catholic area in Brooklyn. We could open another storefront six or seven blocks away in East New York, which is heavily Negro and Puerto Rican. East New York is attuned to a totally different point of view; there's only one Republican organization in the whole area, and there is simply no contact with the Negro neighborhoods.

"We could play this any way we wanted to. The guy working for Lindsay was clean; he had no commitments. In the Negro neighborhoods, we could recruit Negro volunteers and distribute Lindsay literature aimed for a Negro audience. In Cypress Hills, we could go another way. We could distribute Lindsay literature aimed at the problems those people were thinking about—the city's fiscal condition and schools. And we weren't bound by the ideas coming out of the storefronts in the Negro areas. In other words, we could take advantage of ethnic breaks."

There's a celebrated area in central Flatbush called The Junction. Most of the people living in it are Jewish-liberal, but there is also a significant belt of conservatives (most of them, once again, Irish Catholics). "In this area," says Blum, with his usual candor, "we could turn and work both sides of the street. In fact, we could work with almost everyone. The Republican organization couldn't be that flexible, and anyway it hardly existed. It had nothing to offer, and I doubt if, even during the campaign, the clubhouse was open more than one night a week. But we were able to work with the Democrats; we could move to the right of the Democrats. We could even appeal to the conservatives and say that a vote for Buckley was really just a vote for Beame." *

Issues were once again important, as they have been in every campaign we have examined. The fact that Bob Price is not much of a believer in polling doesn't mean he isn't oriented toward issues. It's simply that he believes—rightly or wrongly—that he and the people working for him can sense issues intuitively as well as polls can turn them up scientifically. In Lindsay's Seventeenth District, for example, Price and his people could collect a reasonable cross section of complaints in a day or two; the district, geographically, was that small. And Oregon is a reasonably homogeneous kind of place Besides, in Oregon, Price worked just one issue—Rockefeller cared enough to come.

A mayoralty election is a local election, even in a place the size of New York. Voters are interested in local problems.

"The newspapers kept saying Lindsay wasn't talking about the issues," Bob Blum said. "But the thinking about issues in mid-Manhattan is shaped by *The New York Times*. These are people who really worry about bond issues. These are people like those who live in Peter Cooper Village who think of themselves as political scientists.

"But that's not really New York. Out in Mill Basin there's nothing bigger than paving the streets. And the guy who promises to move along on street paving is going to win there.

"We faced issues like the outrage of people who lived in a housing development and had to send their kids across a busy street to a new school. That busy street had no lights,

---

* In fact, of course, a vote for Buckley was often a vote for Lindsay. That's because Buckley pulled so many of his votes from conservative Democrats, many of them Irish Catholics.

no blinkers, not even a stop sign. The kids were flocking across this street, right into all that traffic, and the mothers were worried. And then it happened: In the second week of school, a truck killed a kid.

"Lindsay's schedule was kept flexible just to meet this sort of thing. In forty-eight hours we had him at our storefront there. There were maybe 500 people there to listen to him. He climbed up on a chair and said, 'I know about your problem and I've written a letter to the traffic department. I promise you that if I'm elected I'll get a traffic light in for you.'" The light, as a matter of fact, was installed shortly after Lindsay's inauguration.

These local issues were turned up systematically and handled in an organized fashion. The "Eristoff Manual" laid it out:

It is extremely important that one person in your assembly district be known as the "issues" man. His job is to find as many local problems as exist and see to it that the candidates know about them prior to their campaigning. This will include such matters as that there are not enough street lights on the corner, or that there are not enough parks or playgrounds in the area. Our goal is to show the voters in this city that our candidates mean business and are determined to learn about the city and to solve the problems on a local basis.

Words like crime, housing, education, parks and hospitals are generalities. Learn the specific problems within these and other categories.

Get a writer or local enthusiast—activist type, a member of the local planning board, for example—who is well versed in community problems, and tell him to identify 10 local issues of extreme importance to residents of the community. He can be the "temporary issues co-chairman." He should put together a "local issues committee."

We'll provide "local issue forms" which can be used to identify these issues with suggested solutions. These should be

sent to Bill Tobin at city HQ, through the borough co-ordinators, who will pass them on to the research group. The facts
will be researched and checked. Occasionally, HQ Research
will contact you directly for up-to-date information on pertinent issues. . . . Ultimately, a considered position will be
reached, which will be submitted to JVL for consideration
and action.

JVL must be briefed as to local issues before walking
through the area.

Lindsay's handling of these purely neighborhood issues
did not, of course, get much, if any, attention in the city's
daily newspapers. They did, however, get mention in the
city's dozens of little weekly newspapers. Lindsay's concern
for neighborhood problems was also spread by word of
mouth. No one can say with precision what all of this meant
in terms of votes, but I would guess it was significant, especially when one considers that New York has long been bur-
dened with a heavy-handed bureaucracy that studies, studies,
and then studies some more, and rarely does much of anything to solve these aggravating, petty problems that frus-
trate millions of New Yorkers. Everyone likes to talk about
alienation these days—the alienated Negro, the alienated intellectual—and sometimes one wonders: Can everyone be
that alienated? But in New York City, there can be little
doubt of it: People were alienated in 1965, and Lindsay's
deeply personal, "retail" campaign no doubt drew an emotional response.* The question we shall raise later is whether
the technique he employed was the most effective one.

---

* Lindsay is, of course, a showman and a bit of a ham. He likes
to be the center of attention. But he has courage, and his motivation
is surely sincere. He walked the streets of New York all during the
long, hot summer of 1967, showing his concern for people, and New
York did not become a Newark or a Detroit. He avoided a problem;
he didn't solve one. But that in itself was a gratifying achievement.

In making this kind of appeal, Lindsay was simply shot full of luck, for he had no competition.

First, there was little Abe Beame, a man of integrity and even some ability, despite his backing by Steingut, Buckley, and Powell. But Beame's background is a bookkeeper's; he likes to consider rows and rows of figures; he is not comfortable with rows of people. Nor is he comfortable with ideas. Beyond that, he couldn't give an effective speech.

He had won the primary because he could argue that he was the only Democrat running in it who had publicly and regularly challenged Wagner's leadership. That claim, as we shall soon see, was nicely rebutted by the Lindsay researchers. But it worked in the primary; he had an issue; he had organizational support; and he was Jewish in a city that is one-third Jewish. Running with him was Frank O'Connor, a gentle and popular Irishman, and the irrepressible Mario Procaccino, whose campaign malapropisms are now legend.

Beame's original pitch in the general election was his boast that he could bring businesslike government to New York City. That, however, was something less than inspiring. His managers sensed the problem and took a new direction —that Beame was a member of a great team that also included the likes of Bobby Kennedy, Hubert Humphrey, and Lyndon Johnson. It was an ancient device—an attempt to tie a little man to the coattails of bigger men. It doesn't very often work; it didn't, as things turned out, work for Beame.

It's hard to believe, but once again the Democrats made the same mistake—they misread the polls. The first reports put Beame comfortably ahead of Lindsay. The follow-up reports showed a drop-off, but nothing very significant. And so the Beame team (the phrase is theirs) relaxed.

Of all Beame's advisers, apparently only Bobby Kennedy sensed trouble ahead. Maas and Thimmesch, in their campaign analysis, report that Kennedy attended a strategy session on October 10 and listened patiently as the Beame managers indulged in self-congratulation. "You're ahead now," Kennedy told them, "but you're drifting. If you don't have two or three positive programs ready when the newspaper strike is over, you'll drift right out of the election." Somebody, Maas and Thimmesch continue, suggested that things weren't so bad; that Beame already had 60 percent of the Negro vote. "He should have 80 percent!" Kennedy replied.

The Beame team also made one of the monumental blunders of modern campaign history. They leaked a story that Hubert Humphrey, scheduled to deliver a speech on October 26—a week shy of Election Day—would bring with him a ringing endorsement from the President. That, of course, was desperately needed to back up Beame's principal argument that he was, in fact, a member of the big-time Democratic team. But, after this buildup, Humphrey lamely explained in front of an audience of eager, expectant Democrats that all he had brought was the President's "warm regards."

Then, there was Bill Buckley. In trying to describe Buckley as a candidate, one gropes for words. Beame came close to being inarticulate. Buckley was articulate to the point of incomprehensibility; his vocabulary is enough to stun a lexicographer. And then, there were his singular mannerisms. Beame merely shuffled on a public platform, but Buckley gyrated. He would fold his arms across his chest and then squeeze himself in a bear hug. He'd stretch out his arms until you thought you could hear the joints crack, and then he'd squeeze and unsqueeze his fingers. Finally, in what was almost an alarming phenomenon, he would jam his thumbs inside his belt and push his trousers down around his hips. The effect was so startling that many people in the audience, women especially, would giggle, nervously. And, of course, his voice: It was (it is) Westchester County, Groton, Hyde Park, an amalgam recited by Henry Higgins.

Buckley, in his sadly unamusing book *The Unmaking of a Mayor,* argues that he seriously tried to project important issues in his campaign. Principally, he says, he tried to protest a New York tradition in which political leaders play off one group, or bloc, against another. He tried to argue that people should be considered as individuals. But Buckley is a fetishist—about words. Whenever he had the chance to be simperingly smart aleck, he took it. His contempt for little, defenseless Abe Beame and serious, cliché-prone John Lindsay was manifest. It was too much. Thousands of voters, originally bemused by Buckley, ultimately became just plain bored.*

We have already seen how Lindsay tried to capitalize on local, neighborhood issues. Just as well organized was his handling of city-wide issues.

This part of the campaign was supervised by George Lindsay, the candidate's brother, and by John Deardourff, one of the best political researchers in the business. Deardourff holds a master's degree in international studies from the Fletcher School of Law and Diplomacy. He was one of two key men lent to Lindsay by the Rockefeller organization

---

* There is, too, the irony of the cool, sophisticated Buckley and the angry, florid, bigoted New Yorkers who were his chief boosters. The people who went to his rallies and distributed his buttons and broadsides were alienated, with a vengeance. For conservatives, the gap between ideological creativity at the top and ideological interpretation at the bottom continues to be a challenge.

(the other was press secretary Harry O'Donnell).* It was Deardourff who supervised the "negative research" on Barry Goldwater in 1964; in 1965 he did the same sort of "negative research" into Abe Beame's background.

A group of young volunteers—most of them reform Democrats—was assigned to check out Beame's boast that he had been the one Democrat who regularly opposed Mayor Wagner. These volunteers noted that Beame had been city comptroller for four years. In that time, they figured, he had voted thousands of times as a member of the policy-making Board of Estimate. So the question: How many of those votes were anti-Wagner?

It was an immense amount of work, but it was finished. The volunteers found that Beame had voted 15,312 times in those four years at Board of Estimate meetings. And how many of those votes were anti-Wagner? Just four!

A devastating finding, but how best to capitalize on it?

The traditional way would be to write a press release: "John V. Lindsay, candidate for mayor, charged today that his opponent, Abraham D. Beame, voted against Mayor Robert F. Wagner only four times in four years."

"The effective marketing of this kind of material," says Deardourff, "is just as important as its content. Had we released our findings in the dead of night for A.M. release in the papers they never would have surfaced.

"So what we did was to prepare 'visuals' proving our point, and then called a press conference. It was all aimed for television, and it worked. We had a huge posterboard mounted in front of the cameras. All you could see were the words, 'The Odds Are'; the rest was covered over. Lindsay, who is very good at this sort of thing, began talking while

---

* After the 1966 Rockefeller election, Deardourff became a principal partner in Campaign Consultants, Inc. (see Chapter Two).

the suspense over that posterboard began building. He talked about the extensive research we had done and he said that Beame had been trying to run away from his involvement with the Wagner administration. We teased them along. Finally, as the cameras were grinding away and as Gabe Pressman [New York's Huntley-Brinkley] was eating it all up, Lindsay stripped away the paper. Now it read, 'The Odds Are 15,312 to 4 That Beame Will Be Just Another Wagner.' The posterboard also said that Beame, based on his voting record, was 99 and 44/100 percent pure Wagner because he had gone along with Wagner that much of the time. The effect was just devastating. You just wouldn't believe how much free television time we got on that one. The stuff appeared on all the news shows."

That wasn't the end of it. Within hours, brochures were coming off the presses for distribution in all parts of the city. Distribution points, of course, were the storefronts. The language in the brochures was a trifle stronger. "The truth is that Abe Beame is 99 and 44/100 percent pure Wagner—with the most insidious political machine since Boss Tweed thrown in to boot." The additional material was that hyperbole about Tweed. This brochure and all the rest, incidentally, had an interesting quote attached: "Sometimes party loyalty asks too much." It was attributed to John F. Kennedy.

Literature was a very large item in the Lindsay campaign. No one really knows now how much of it, or how many individual items, was distributed. But the literature included this flyer: "John Lindsay, candidate for mayor, promises the No. 2 bus will run on 7th Avenue every 10 minutes when I am Mayor." The flyers were distributed at appropriate bus stops.

George Lindsay and Deardourff supervised the preparation of 17 issues papers, most of which were aimed at *The*

New York Times audience. Each paper was originally prepared by a task force of volunteer experts. It gave important people a role in the campaign that at least appeared to be important. Perhaps the papers were important by themselves —it is, after all, important to convince opinion-makers that your candidate is serious and thoughtful—but, then again, it may have been the way the papers were peddled that made them unusually convincing.

Once again, press conferences were scheduled. And the material was presented with visual aids. At the press conference dealing with the paper on crime and law enforcement, for example, photographic blowups of advanced equipment used in the Chicago Police Department headquarters were shown. At the press conference dealing with parks and recreation, a model was displayed of a floating swimming pool that the paper was recommending be built on the Hudson River.

"Almost every one of these papers was presented in this way to make it appealing for the television cameras," says Deardourff. "As a result, we got extraordinary coverage. And we also got favorable editorial comment. Sometimes *The New York Times* was unhappy, but usually it acknowledged we were being thoughtful and serious. I remember they were unhappy with our fiscal paper, but that was because the *Times*'s solution is always to raise taxes and we were in no position to propose that."

That, then, was how it was. John Lindsay was elected mayor. The vote totals: Lindsay, 1,166,915; Beame, 1,030,771; Buckley, 339,127.

II—How It Might Have Been

After the election, Bob Price told me that he was never terribly worried. "I felt," he said, "that all we had to do was push the right buttons and we'd be home." But look again at those final returns. Beame and Buckley combined received 1,369,898 votes, 202,983 *more* than Lindsay. Lindsay, in other words, won with less than a majority.

It is no doubt churlish to knock success—Lindsay, after all, is mayor of New York today. But it is my own judgment —subjective, intuitive, and related not at all to the new politics—that he should have been swept into office in a landslide.

Just consider what he had going for him. The incumbent Wagner administration was struggling; it was forlorn. The voters were ready to turn it out. Then the Democrats chose Abe Beame—Abe Beame!—as their candidate. Beame was forlorn from the outset of the campaign. He was a bookkeeper in a city that desperately wanted a leader. If that weren't enough, Bill Buckley entered the race, and immediately began appealing to conservative Democrats. Lindsay was fresh and handsome and vigorous. He had immense campaign resources, including an open Rockefeller family bankroll. He had been endorsed by the Liberal Party, and his ticket included both a Liberal and a Democrat. Fusion is an ancient tradition in New York City, and Lindsay's ticket looked like a fine fusion effort. To be sure, Democrats outnumber Republicans in New York by better than 3 to 1, but Lindsay wasn't running as a Republican. He owed nothing to the creaking Republican organization, and he gave it nothing.

It was for all these reasons, and more, that most experts predicted at the campaign's outset that Lindsay would win with relative ease. But he didn't—and I suggest it was because the campaign run in his behalf was wasteful, inefficient, and old-fashioned.

How could Lindsay have done better? By using some of the new techniques we have been discussing. Which techniques? If you've come this far, I'm sure you can make some smart guesses. But let's tick off the possibilities:

1. Good polling. Lindsay was a new face to most New Yorkers. To a lesser extent, so was Beame. And Buckley was a totally unexpected commodity. Good polling would have determined voter attitudes and perceptions about all three men. Fred Currier's semantic-differential approach would have been highly significant, I believe. What were the strengths of the three candidates? What were the weaknesses? There were all kinds of speculation about Buckley's candidacy. Good polling would have supplied some decision-making rationale. Polling would also have helped in determining the nature of those issues that had citywide significance. Seventeen substantive-issues papers were prepared, you will remember. I suspect some of those issues were inconsequential. I suspect, too, that others were neglected that could have been of consequence. Polling would have permitted scientific judgment, up to a point. Polling could also have been used to determine with a higher degree of accuracy the issues that had narrower significance. I don't say that polls could have been taken in each Assembly District, but I think polling could have been directed at least to each borough.

2. Good television. Consider, once again, that Lindsay was a new face to most New Yorkers. I would suspect, too, that polling would have turned up the significant fact that many New Yorkers had a blurred, fleeting impression that Lindsay was a lightweight and something of a Social Register dabbler. In Pennsylvania, Milton Shapp was a new face too. He was introduced to the voters in a brilliantly produced thirty-minute documentary. A similar documentary, I suggest, would have been even more successful in New York City. More successful because there was more curiosity about Lind-

say than there had been about Shapp. More successful because Lindsay, visually, is much more attractive than Shapp. The theme of a Lindsay documentary might even have been similar—The Man Against the Machine. Such a documentary, given saturation coverage early in the campaign, would have introduced Lindsay to the voters and established his theme quickly and through a medium in which the opposition couldn't talk back.

There was in the Lindsay campaign no need to produce the kind of spot television that Rockefeller used in the early stages of his campaign. But I think the kind of hard-hitting television that Rockefeller used late in his campaign would have been wonderfully effective for Lindsay. One obvious possibility: Spot commercials attacking Beame's 99 44/100 pure Wagnerian record. The possibilities are almost endless. Because of its retail nature, the Lindsay campaign started on a high note, sagged badly in those middle weeks when the newspapers were on strike, and then just barely surfaced again in the final week or two. A carefully scheduled television campaign would have gone a long way toward avoiding that kind of problem.

3. Direct mail. The Lindsay managers were quite correct in assuming that neighborhood issues were just as important, and probably more important, than the so-called *New York Times* issues. But the storefront technique, I would argue, was not the way to hammer home those issues. Direct mail was the technique that cried out to be used. Consider, as just one possibility, the situation we discussed in Brooklyn's Fifty-second Assembly District. Ira Kellman, the storefront manager there, was especially proud of signing up Rabbi Schrage. People, Kellman said, saw the rabbi working in the headquarters. But how many people really saw him there? I visited that headquarters on two separate days,

and hardly anyone came in to visit on either occasion. People rushed by on the street outside, and no more than one out of five bothered to glance inside. I very much doubt that substantial numbers of Jewish voters ever learned of Rabbi Schrage's contribution. They all would have known about it if letters had been mailed—personal letters, addressed individually, and signed by the rabbi. Perhaps such a mailing would have been too narrow to be economical. But a mailing in which a group of community leaders joined as sponsors surely would have been within reason.

Or take another example. Robert Blum stressed Lindsay's quick response when a child was killed on a busy street where parents had been agitating for a traffic light. Lindsay appeared at the storefront in that neighborhood within forty-eight hours and spoke to a group of five hundred people. Those people, naturally, told others. Besides that, handbills were distributed. But, I suspect, thousands of voters still remained ignorant of Lindsay's concern. Direct mail might have informed them all.

So much, then, for the obvious, and neglected, possibilities—polling, television, direct mail.

The money that was poured into the storefronts—it was almost $1,000,000, remember—would have been more than enough to cover them all. Perhaps there might even have been enough left over to permit the use of other techniques —data processing, for a major example. A successful direct-mail campaign, in fact, would almost require some data processing. Another possibility: those tape-recorded telephone messages used so successfully by the Romney organization in Michigan.

I am not suggesting that everything the Lindsay managers attempted was wasteful or old-fashioned. I think, as a matter of fact, that the storefront technique, used in moderation and with more direction, has some validity. It occurs to me that storefronts could have been restricted to those parts of the city where ticket-splitting was significant, as determined by the use of those techniques developed in Michigan. And most impressive was Lindsay's ability to appear regularly —and favorably—on television news shows.

On balance, however, the Lindsay campaign was an anachronism. He almost lost an election that should have been a smashing victory. If he had won the kind of victory that I think was within his grasp, I suspect that he might have emerged as a contender for his party's presidential nomination in 1968.

To be sure, speculation. Let us now conclude by speculating some more—on what the new methodology means to American politics, and where it is taking us.

8

CONCLUSION

"Put on a fight," old Clem Whitaker said. And if you can't do that, "Put on a show." How far have we really come from those days?

In some ways, no distance at all; in others, a millennium.

We must grant quite a bit to Whitaker and Baxter. They were the first to see how elections could be won on direct appeal to the voters through the mass media. They proved that elections could be won without regular party organization. But, of course, they proved their point in California, where Hiram Johnson's reforms had effectively destroyed party organization as most of us think of it. Whitaker and Baxter, in effect, filled a vacuum. Though they were private campaign managers, they became a quasi-political organization themselves.

The Whitaker and Baxter innovations did not spread out of California because regular party organizations were still entrenched in many states. As a matter of fact, the Whitaker and Baxter way of doing things went into dramatic decline even in California after Clem Whitaker's death. Spencer and Roberts, as we have seen, are just beginning now to catch up.

Whitaker and Baxter were pioneers, and it is only now—in 1968—that other campaign managers are blazing new trails. The professional manager has finally arrived, in California and almost everywhere else. Within five years, I should think, most major political campaigns in this country will be managed by these new professionals.

Even as this was being written, the professional managers were continuing to demonstrate what the new techniques could accomplish. Sandy Weiner, a professional political manager, and his client, Pete McCloskey, defeated Shirley Temple Black—little Shirley Temple!—in a congressional primary campaign in California. It was the same Sandy Weiner who managed George Murphy's successful campaign for the United States Senate, and it was Murphy who encouraged Mrs. Black to run for Congress.

The success of Murphy and the failure of Shirley Temple tell us something. Murphy, for all his Hollywood background, was knowledgeable about politics; he had, in fact, once been Republican state chairman. Shirley Temple was ignorant of politics. Murphy was willing to face the voters and the press; Shirley Temple was not. "Wide public exposure is the only way a movie star can combat the feeling among voters that he doesn't have the background for public office," Weiner said after McCloskey's primary victory. "She [Shirley Temple] was too cold, too well rehearsed. People remembered her as dancing little Shirley Temple. Then they saw a nice-appearing matron who was too staged, too stuffy. With Murphy and Reagan, people were charmed. They came away saying 'Wow.' With Shirley, they just came away."

It takes a little more than a pretty face and a show-biz background to win elections, despite the lamentations of critics like Daniel Boorstin. To win, a candidate must be reasonably credible. Good management, of course, can help to create that kind of credibility. But the candidate still must have something. Shirley Temple was not credible, and I doubt that superior management (which she didn't have) could have made her so.

Even more impressive was the Republican sweep in New Jersey. The state organization there hired Campaign Consultants, Inc.—perhaps the hottest of all the new management firms—to direct a consolidated campaign for the state legislature. Before the election, the Democrats controlled both houses of the legislature by margins of 2 to 1. After the election (in November of 1967), Republicans controlled both houses by margins of 3 to 1. CCI also managed the Republican campaign in Bergen County in northern New Jersey. Before that election, Democrats held all five seats in the state senate, nine of ten seats in the state assembly, and all three positions on the county board of freeholders. The Republicans, under CCI's tutelage, won them all in a clean sweep.

We need not, then, labor the point: The new techniques as practiced by these professional managers win elections. The old order finally has changed. The traditional party organizations can no longer win elections when opposed by the new managers and the new techniques. When these organizations do win—as in New Jersey—it is because they have adopted the new techniques and the new managers. These winning organizations are the ones that admit they need professional help, and go out and pay for it.

The explanation for the steady deterioration of the traditional party organization is best told by demographers. They simply point to the statistics. In mid-November of

1967, the nation's population passed the 200,000,000 mark, double the figure in 1915. In 1967, the median age for all Americans was 27.7; in 1949, it was 30. In 1949, 34 percent of all Americans lived in the big cities; in 1967, that figure had dropped to 30 percent. At the same time, the suburban percentage climbed from 24 to 34. In 1949, only 34 percent of Americans over 25 had completed four years of high school; that figure had jumped to 50 percent in 1967. In 1967, median family income was $7,436; in 1949, the comparable figure (in 1967 dollars) was $4,230.

Americans in 1967 were more numerous, younger, more suburban, better educated, and wealthier. They were also more mobile and less parochial. No organization can hope to maintain unquestioning loyalty over this kind of constituency.

The new political technology doesn't essentially change the climate of American politics, not at least at the outset. What it does do is take advantage of the fundamental changes that are occurring. In some instances, as we have seen, it takes a very sizable advantage.

"Both parties," says Walter DeVries, "need campaigns that are rational in the way they handle the candidates' time, the campaign resources, the issues, and the public-opinion polls." This is the technologists' creed: that they are simply making politics a rational exercise. And by doing so they are improving the public debate and providing better-equipped public leaders.

This *is* something new. Whitaker and Baxter did not base their decisions upon empirical data. They relied primarily upon intuition, which was often—given their experience—pretty accurate.

The idea of rational decision-making is the major factor that unites all the new political technologists. Rational is the key word. Rational decisions. Rational issues. Rational campaign itineraries. Rational television. Rational literature. The technologists don't want to take a single step in the dark.

But rational for whom? For the candidate, of course. Up to a point, this is fine. No candidate should be irrational. It's a danger to us all when a major candidate badly misjudges the voters' mood. This, of course, is precisely what happened in 1964, when the Goldwater partisans actually believed in their southern strategy. They were even impressed by pro-Goldwater sentiment as reflected in, of all places, letters to the nation's newspaper editors. The new politics should tend to eliminate this kind of irrational behavior.

But that's not really the point. The problem here, it seems to me, is not so much the *input* of the new technology; it's the *output*. It's not, in other words, what the politicians learn from this new science; it's what they do with that learning.

If they so desire, these new managers—acting rationally from their point of view all the while—can play upon the voters like virtuosos. They can push a pedal here, strike a chord there. And, presumably, they can get precisely the response they seek.

We have in the course of this book studied several case histories, and I don't suppose many people would argue that any of these candidates who have been helped by the new politics have been evil men. Most of them, in fact, have been exceptionally qualified. But I think we can note some of their output—and be alarmed.

In Michigan, five good Democratic congressmen were turned out of office by five faceless Republicans, thanks to superior techniques. Robert Griffin, a conservative, was made to appear a moderate. And G. Mennen Williams was pushed by the new technology far to the left of where he actually stood. From a Republican management point of view, it was all quite rational. In California, it was rational for Spencer and Roberts to excuse Ronald Reagan's ignorance about state issues by noting he was a "citizen politician." In New York, it was a rational decision to have Nelson Rockefeller destroy—utterly destroy—a gentle and since opponent. In Arkansas, surely it was rational to gull thousands of voters with computer-printed "personal" letters from Winthrop Rockefeller. We might remember what Marion Burton said: "What's the difference between me sitting down and signing letters or me authorizing a computer runoff of the same letters?"

It was rational, but was it ethical?

Of course not.

So what should be done about it?

Understand it. Deplore it. Raise hell about it.

It is deplorable that so much of the output of the new technology is questionable or unethical. It is just as deplorable that hardly anyone raises hell about it. No newspaper in Arkansas challenged Rockefeller for those computer-printed letters. No newspaper even noted what was happening. In New York, presumably a more sophisticated state, no newspaper that I know about challenged the unfairness—the downright dishonesty—of so much of Nelson Rockefeller's last-stage material.

Each of these new-style campaigns is a little like a magician's act. What you see is the candidate out there on the stump, delivering speeches and making statements. It is almost exclusively this high-level campaign that the reporters and commentators observe. But what the reporters and commentators don't see—what they don't report or assess—is that hand under the table, selling the voters through the mass media in their homes. I would suggest that this second campaign is just as important as the first. Probably more important, for the dirt is usually found under the table.

There is, of course, nothing new about political dirt. Opponents said George Washington wanted to be a king. Jefferson's opponents said he was the son of a half-breed squaw mother and a mulatto father. A Senate committee actually met to consider charges that Lincoln's wife was a Confederate agent.

What is different is that the dirt these days is usually part of this second, and largely unobserved, campaign, while in days gone by it was all part of one campaign. To this extent, the new techniques are responsible for a new and more subtle kind of political dirt.

I suspect, however, that this is a short-term problem. As these new techniques become more and more familiar, the ordinary checks and balances probably will come into balance. The problem will continue to exist—it always has —but it will be recognized for what it is. If nothing else, I should hope that this book might hasten that day of reckoning.

There is another problem growing out of unfamiliarity that may also be short term—the imbalance between the Democrats and the Republicans in seizing upon the new techniques. It is a fact that the Republicans have preempted the new technology. In this book, we have considered the work of only one Democratic technologist—Joe Napolitan. That is no accident; it's simply because there are no others, none, at least, of the quality we have been seeking.

I have no doubt that the post-1964 upsurge in Republican strength is at least partly attributable to that party's employment of these new campaign methods. Ray Bliss has been preaching the new politics at the Republican National Committee. The Democratic National Committee, meanwhile, has been adding up its payroll on a computer, and doing little else. The White House, where any incumbent party's power lies, is ill-prepared to compete at this level. President Johnson has yet to demonstrate that he even understands the purposes of political polls. It may be that Larry O'Brien, the postmaster general, understands the new politics, but he is in no position *now* to do much about it. There is always, of course, Robert F. Kennedy, and anyone who knows much about him must believe that he appreciates the changing requirements of modern political campaigning. But he is biding his time.

I am sure the Democrats ultimately will catch on and the balance will be restored. Meanwhile, however, the Republicans will continue to win elections they should, by rights, be losing. When the Democrats do catch up, we shall probably see campaigns like the general election in Pennsylvania. There, Milton Shapp, managed by Joe Napolitan, was matched against Raymond Shafer, supported by an alert Republican organization. It was an expensive, hard-hitting campaign in which the man who ordinarily should have won—Shafer—did in fact win.

But there are more fundamental questions, whose outlines can be only dimly sketched. Perhaps these can be summed up in the question: Is the new politics essentially antiparty? I suspect that it may be and that we are entering an era of personalized politics.

Consider some of the case histories we have studied— Shapp in Pennsylvania, Romney in Michigan, Nelson Rockefeller in New York, Winthrop Rockefeller in Arkansas. Not one of these men is an old-fashioned party loyalist. Each created his own campaign organization and hired his own specialists. As we have seen, some of these personal organizations actually became substitutes for the official party organization, especially in Michigan and New York.

Candidates who cannot afford to build personal organizations, or who don't have the time or inclination to do so, are now able to hire political-management firms. I think these firms are also antiparty because they, too, tend to become substitutes for regular party machinery. The professional managers are mercenaries; they are willing to go almost anywhere for a buck. So far, most of these mercenaries have restricted their activities to one party or the other. I can see a day coming when firms will be organized that will work for either party, just as political pollsters already do.

What we are seeing is the steady development of two essentially antiparty phenomena—the personal organization and the political-management firm. And, I submit, we are only at the threshold of a sweeping political trend.

Soon, I think, we shall begin to see a melding of these two phenomena. That is to say, some candidates will build personal organizations and, additionally, hire management or consulting firms. This sort of thing will become more commonplace as management or consulting firms are organized as specialists. For example, Joe Napolitan and F. Clifton White (who is best known for his work in winning the Republican nomination for Goldwater in 1964) have organized a firm that specializes in data processing. Other firms, I feel certain, will be organized to specialize in, say, television or direct mail. The Simulmatics Corp., as we have seen, already exists to specialize in simulation.

There is already, then, a trend toward personalization of the American political system. In the next few years this trend will quicken as more personal organizations are developed and as these management and consulting firms expand. And, as personal politics expands, party politics will almost surely contract.

This could lead to a fragmentation of the two-party system. Conceivably, individuals could form personal organizations, hire mercenaries, and campaign outside the structure of either party. This, of course, would be wholly outside the American political tradition. But I don't think it will happen. It seems to me that the tendency is for these candidates relying upon the new technology to work within one party or the other, even if they do not maintain a sense of party loyalty. Milton Shapp is a good example of what I have in mind. Ten years ago Shapp could not have sought high office; it would never have occurred to him that he could win the Democratic nomination. The organization wouldn't have permitted it. But it occurred to Shapp in 1966 that he could employ these new techniques to defeat the Democratic organization in a Democratic primary. By now, that lesson must be clear to countless others. Thus, I think, party fragmentation in days to come will be especially significant at the party primary level.

The same situation exists in presidential politics. Candidates for party presidential nominations will, I think, continue to work within the two-party structure. But, more and more, they will rely upon personal organization and professional assistance. Not long ago, it would have been inconceivable to think that an incumbent President could be denied renomination. It is still unlikely—but the possibility, thanks to the new technology, becomes less remote every year. At this writing, for example, it seems to me entirely possible that Robert F. Kennedy could seriously challenge Lyndon Johnson for the 1968 nomination, if he chose to do so and if he employed all the techniques we have been discussing.

Much of this speculation rests solidly upon a presumption—that the regular party organizations will be unwilling or unable to seize upon these new techniques themselves. It is not, I admit, an entirely comfortable presumption.

Yet, consider Nelson Rockefeller's 1966 campaign for governor. In describing that campaign, we noted that the new politics—so successfully employed by Rockefeller—requires money, talent, and time. In all three, where does the advantage lie—with a Rockefeller or with a political organization?

Money: No organization can hope to match a Rockefeller in fund raising. A Rockefeller needs only to write a check.

Talent: Money can hire talent, and a Rockefeller or a Kennedy and maybe even a Romney has that kind of money. But more than that, these new technologists seek power. I suspect they get more satisfaction—more sense of power—working with a man of ability and potential than they do working for an institutionalized organization.

Time: Personal organizations have the time they need to develop a new-style campaign, and sometimes—as we have seen—that kind of campaign takes months to put together. Regular party organizations frequently stand aside during a contested primary and only go to work thereafter. Then, of course, it's often too late to develop a winning campaign.

We are now, of course, approaching the nub of the problem—the way the new techniques and men of power and wealth seek out one another. Together, in the right hands, they become a juggernaut.

In a democracy with a tradition (if not always a history) of equality of opportunity, this is of course unacceptable. Somehow, the odds favoring the man of wealth must be evened.

But how? I can see no way except a government-operated program of subsidies. Candidates for all federal offices and, I think, most important state offices, should be given significant help. And not only in the general elections, but in the primaries, for—in a point often overlooked—it is in the primaries that personal wealth usually counts most.

I would suggest that consideration should be given to a matching-grant system, starting in the primaries. To receive a subsidy, a potential candidate would be required to round up supporting signatures, the number depending upon the importance of the office. He would then be required to raise from his followers—a broad cross section of followers—a stipulated amount of money, the amount again depending upon the office. Such a system would, I think, help to solve the problem inherent in most subsidy formulas—that they would tend to turn elections into frivolous free-for-alls. Other, and larger, matching grants would be available to the primary winners in the general election.

Any such program should also include a leather-tough campaign-spending provision. Hardly anyone now reports campaign expenditures accurately; it is simply a national scandal.

There may be some virtue, too, in considering, as an alternate, a program providing subsidies for campaign services, paid to those supplying the services. Such a program might better tie into the realities of the new politics. Television stations, for example, might be reimbursed for supplying equal time to qualifying candidates in both primary and general elections. The amount of equal time would, once again, depend upon the importance of the office being sought. I would also argue that radio and television stations should be required to set aside *some* prime time for political commercials. Going a step farther, perhaps advertising agencies meeting minimal requirements could be reimbursed for preparing television commercials and programs, and other materials, for qualifying candidates. This kind of subsidy has merit, I think, because simply making free time available is really no equalizer. Bad television, as we have seen, is worse than no television at all.

Direct mail is a key part of most modern political campaigns, and I can see no reason why qualifying candidates could not be immediately extended some free mailing privileges. Perhaps those same advertising agencies could be paid for preparing the content of the mailings.

Programs of this kind are needed—now. But let us be honest; no program is going to eliminate all the rich man's advantages. Money is power, and more money is more power.

What is probably needed almost as much as anything else is a sense of outrage on the part of the American voters. So far, hardly anyone seems to object to Nelson Rockefeller spending vast sums of his own money to elect himself. But voters do seem to mind when men of more moderate means are forced, by actual necessity, to beg for money to pay their bills. A change in public attitude is already long overdue. With such a change might come an increased willingness on the part of Americans of ordinary means to contribute to the campaigns of like-minded men of moderate means.

It is a ponderous cliché to note that a successful democracy requires a reasonably alert and intelligent citizenry. Nonetheless, it is so. Until now, the American voter has been as responsible as he has had to be, and not much more.

And it is to him that these new techniques are being directed. A pessimist would suggest that it is simply too much. Most voters aren't all that interested in their political system. They're struggling to make a living, to raise their children, to pay *their* bills. So they will be polled and simulated and prodded and pushed.

I hope the pessimists are wrong. We have been dehumanized enough as it is, what with credit cards and computerized bank statements and digit dialing and zip codes.

Politics once was something akin to good clean fun. It was the great American game, and we could all play it. Sure it was dirty. And, to be sure, all too often it was dishonest. But it was *human* and it was nonscientific. Now, if the pessimists are right, politics, like so much else, will be dehumanized too. Like Knocko McCormack, most of us will be put on ice.

SOURCE NOTES

CHAPTER TWO: Most of the material in this chapter, as in all those that follow, was obtained largely through personal interview. I am especially indebted to Bill Roberts and Stu Spencer for all the many hours of valuable time they made available to me. My first story about their partnership appeared in the *National Observer* in April of 1964. The material about Whitaker and Baxter is another matter. I have relied extensively on Stanley Kelley's *Professional Public Relations and Political Power* (Johns Hopkins, 1966); a series of three articles by Carey McWilliams that appeared in the *Nation* in 1951; an article, "The Influence of Professional Campaign Management Firms in Partisan Elections in California," by Robert J. Pitchell, from the June, 1958, issue of *Western Political Quarterly;* and Irwin Ross's "The Supersalesmen of California Politics: Whitaker and Baxter," an article that appeared in *Harper's Magazine* in July of 1959.

CHAPTER THREE: Joe Napolitan has been wonderfully

helpful, in the preparation of this chapter and in others as well. I have also relied upon his privately circulated, eighty-eight-page Analysis of the 1966 Campaign for Governor of Pennsylvania, a valuable document. Richard Stolley's article that appeared in the May 27, 1966, issue of *Life* magazine was first rate, and it was Stolley's reporting that prompted my own curiosity. My first article about the Shapp campaign appeared in the *National Observer* in September of 1966.

CHAPTER FOUR: Walter D. DeVries of Governor Romney's staff contributed much of his time and resources to the preparation of this chapter. He permitted me to examine the records of the 1966 elections freely, including the polls themselves. Without this data, the chapter would not have been possible. I am indebted to Mr. DeVries for many things, but especially for the fact that he did not quibble about the liberties I took with the information he so graciously supplied. Fred Currier, the Romney organization's pollster, was equally helpful. At one time, he took two full days to instruct me in the art of political polling. Both Currier and DeVries supplied me with lengthy and articulate memoranda describing their work. Other associates of the governor, especially Glen Batchelder, Richard Helmbrecht, and John Boyington, were cordial and informative.

CHAPTER FIVE: Most of the principal campaign advisers to Nelson Rockefeller cooperated in the preparation of this chapter. I should especially mention Dr. William J. Ronan, William L. Pfeiffer, George Hinman, and Les Slote. The people at Jack Tinker & Partners, the advertising agency that worked so brilliantly in the Rockefeller campaign, were enthusiastically helpful. They permitted me to watch all the television commercials they prepared, and made their scripts available as well. Tinker's Jack Conroy gave up much of his time to talk television to me. Jim O'Donnell of Frank O'Connor's staff helped in filling in that side of the picture. My first report about the campaign appeared in the *National Observer* in January of 1967.

CHAPTER SIX: The material about Winthrop Rockefeller's use of data processing was supplied by Charles Nichols, who showed me the actual equipment and tried to tell me how it worked, and Marion Burton. The Republican National Committee's Edward J. Nichols gave an interesting overview. I have also relied upon his fifty-seven-page handbook, *Electronic Data Processing and Politics,* the best (perhaps the only) work of its kind. An off-the-record, day-long seminar attended by politicians and representatives of a large computer-manufacturing firm was also illuminating. A seminar at the Institute of Politics at Harvard University's John Fitzgerald Kennedy School of Government was provocative. Paul Newman, a partner in Datamatics, Inc., described that firm's operations, and supplied interesting documentation. William H. Wilcox showed me how a critical-path method has been applied in politics. Edward L. Greenfield and Alex Bernstein of The Simulmatics Corp. described the simulation process. *Candidates, Issues, and Strategies,* by Ithiel de Sola Pool, Robert P. Abelson, and Samuel Popkin (Massachusetts Institute of Technology, Press Paperback Edition, 1965), reports on the simulation experiment in the 1960 presidential election. My first report on data processing and politics appeared in the *National Observer* in September of 1967.

CHAPTER SEVEN: Though protesting all the way, Robert Price found time to talk about the Lindsay campaign. Robert

M. Blum, my college classmate seventeen years ago, was thoughtful and informative. Constantine Sidamon-Eristoff was kind enough to supply campaign material. John Deardourff, a gentleman and a scholar, taught me about modern political research; no one knows more about it. "The Fight for City Hall: Anatomy of a Victory," by Peter Maas and Nick Thimmesch, a very long article that appeared in the late and lamented *New York* magazine of the *Herald Tribune,* is probably the best published account of the Lindsay campaign, even though it barely mentions the storefront effort. Barbara Carter's *The Road to City Hall* (Prentice-Hall, Inc., 1967) is nicely put but not very instructive. *The Unmaking of a Mayor* (Viking, 1966), by William F. Buckley, Jr., tells more about the author than most people care to know.

INDEX